RUDOLF STEINER
Life, Work, Inner Path
& Social Initiatives

Rudi Lissau

HAWTHORN PRESS

Published by Hawthorn Press,
Bankfield House, 13 Wallbridge, Stroud, GL5 3JA, United Kingdom.

First edition.

Typeset in Plantin by Glevum Graphics, 2 Honyatt Road, Gloucester.

Printed by Billing & Son Limited, Worcester.

British Library Cataloguing in Publication Data

Lissau, Rudi
Rudolf Steiner: his life, work, inner path and social initiatives.
(Social ecology series; 7).
1. Steiner, Rudolf   2. Philosophers – Austria – Biography
I. Title II. Series
193   BP595.S895

ISBN 1 86989 006 X

Dedication

This book is dedicated to my lifelong friend, Hans Schauder. It was his idea that I write a book on Rudolf Steiner, and he encouraged me when I faltered.

Acknowledgements

Dr H. Schauder and Dr A. Welburn were good enough to read the book, chapter by chapter, as it was written. Their advice was most gratefully received, but, occasionally, not acted upon. So it is I who must, of course, take full responsibility for all the shortcomings of the text. Part of the book was also discussed with Diana Harris. Pat Hague typed carefully and at short notice two drafts of the text, and David McGregor, the librarian at Rudolf Steiner House, London was of never-failing help and forbearance. To all of these my heartfelt thanks. A special debt of gratitude is owed to Saul Bellow. He read large parts of the first draft. At his advice certain passages were omitted, others re-arranged and substantial holes filled in. I hope that the second version will please him.

Contents

Stresses and Strains   38
The Spiritual Dimension   39
Faith   45
Everyday Affairs   47
The Lecturer: an Appendix   49
Immediacy   50
Relation to Audience   52

PART II   The Teaching

Chapter Three   *A Philosopher of Freedom*   57

                 Some General Remarks   59

Chapter Four   *Universe, Earth and Man*   62

                 Natural Science and the Science of the Spirit   62
                 Maya   63
                 Man's Cosmic Origin   64
                 Body, Soul and Spirit   66
                 The Four Bodies   68
                 A Provisional Summary   70

Chapter Five   *Christ and the Destiny of Man*   71

                 A Festival of Knowledge   72
                 The Fifth Gospel   73
                 The World in Evolution   74
                 Father and Son   75
                 Jesus and Christ   76
                 The Turning Point of Time   76
                 The Ego: Freedom and Love   78
                 Too Beautiful to be True?   79
                 Karma   80
                 Human Fallibility   80

PART III   The Path

PART IV   Social and Cultural Initiatives

Foreword

The Unheard Cry for Meaning is the title of a book by Victor Frankl, the eminent psychiatrist who survived the hell of Auschwitz. People can cope with any situation provided they see meaning in it. Meaning, alas, is in short supply these days. The churches who used to present us with a meaningful view of existence have lost much of their persuasive power. Reductionist science has been able to destroy the belief of past centuries, but unable to establish any meaning at all. Many contemporaries feel they live in a meaningless world, chance products in a universe without purpose.

This tragic fact set many people on a search of their own and often led them to the ancient wisdom of the East. Thereby they passed by the phenomenon of Rudolf Steiner who in the first quarter of this century spoke about some of his investigations into spiritual matters. His message is addressed to the alienated person of the West who is searching for new directions. One is not asked to abandon one's individuality, but to deepen it, one is not asked to forego one's conscious mind, but to widen it. Most of all: one is not led along a beaten track into a fold, but encouraged to establish one's own authenticity, to be true to one's own experiences, to enter a new sphere of freedom.

Readers are also likely to find surprisingly many and diverse practical propositions concerning social and cultural renewal. These have been of interest also to people who felt unable to relate to Steiner's spiritual awareness.

Rudi Lissau

The Social Ecology Series

The *Social Ecology Series* addresses current social, human, ecological and spiritual questions. A basic approach is that constructive work on such questions requires both inner and outer development – 'as within so without' – a polarity of personal growth and social action.

The books in the series – for example *Social Ecology, Man on the Threshold, Hope, Evolution and Change, Ariadne's Awakening, Dying Forests, Vision in Action* – arise from the work of different groups and networks of people. When this work has reached a certain maturity, people ask for working and study books, which reach beyond the original network.

Developing a series is like bringing up a family – and publishing each book is like enabling a birth to take place. Just as each person has their unique identity, life, tasks, temperament and physique – so each book is like a 'being', with a particular set of tasks.

Rudolf Steiner is no exception. But why a book on Rudolf Steiner in a *Social Ecology Series?* Firstly, many people in the green movement have looked to Steiner's social initiatives in education, agriculture, industry and politics for alternative models – hence the perhaps pejorative description of Steiner as a 'guru of the greens'. Secondly, Steiner built on Goethe's path of the selfless observation of the organic world. He suggested how this sensitised thinking could *both* bring about new insights in ecology (cf. Jochen Bockemühl's *Dying Forests*) *and* could lead to social initiatives. Thirdly, Steiner stressed personal development as *one* way of tackling the social and ecological problems which we face.

By social ecology – literally 'social house wisdom' – is meant both the understanding of the processes of development in the natural, human and social spheres, and the fostering of such development.

Rudolf Steiner could therefore be called a 'social ecologist', and Rudi Lissau's book attempts to describe Steiner both as a spiritual teacher and as a radical social reformer.

Judy and Martin Large, Hawthorn Press

PART I
The Man and His Life

Chapter One
Life

Rudolf Steiner's parents were natives of the *Waldviertel*, a remote part of Lower Austria, not far from the Czech border. No railway had yet opened up this district, and feudal conditions were still strong. Father and mother met as servants of the local landowner, Count Hoyos. The count, however, refused his permission for a marriage and so the two decided not only to leave his service, but also the district in which the noble lord was the main employer. Johann Steiner found work at Austria's Southern Railway which connected Vienna, the capital, with its main port, Trieste. During his time as a railway employee he served at a number of stations, all of which were no more than 40 miles from Vienna. But there was one exception. For a short time he was transferred to Kraljevec, an insignificant village in what is now Northern Yugoslavia. So it came that Rudolf Steiner was born on 27th February 1861 in a Slav environment and not in a German-speaking one, a fact which he considered essential for his life's work.[1]

Early Experiences

The boy must often have felt isolated, set apart from others. In the small village where his father worked there were social stratifications of which he became aware at an early age. The other children belonged to farming families, he was a member of the rural proletariat. The others had their roots firmly in the village, he had intruded on them from the outside. His early clairvoyant experiences increased this feeling of isolation. He described for us only the first of these events. He 'saw' an unknown woman who asked for his help and who later turned out to be a distant relative who had committed suicide at the precise hour at which the boy had become aware of her request. But there must have been many other and poignant experiences so that soon the world fell for him into two parts: the one he could freely talk about and the other he could communicate to nobody. Very early a stubborn streak of independence became manifest. He would not greet his father's superiors and rather preferred to go into hiding. He later admitted that he was also "rather inapproachable for what people generally told him".[2]

This inner isolation went hand in hand with an active involvement in his environment. He worked on the family's smallholding, planted potatoes and helped breeding pigs. On the neighbouring farms there was need for juvenile herdsmen, he picked berries in the forest and fetched water from a particular spring a few miles away, so there was simply no time for play. – In his twenties, somewhat belatedly, he had to learn it in order to play with the four boys whose tutor he was. – All the time he learned: he understood village life in all its social stratifications and the tension between a German-speaking village and the Hungarian authorities mainly in the person of the local priest. He went to school and went to mass, he tried to discover what happened in the near-by factories, he learned how the railway signals worked and how the telegraph functioned. The assistant schoolmaster attracted him through his playing the violin and the piano, and by his gift of drawing. He was intensely interested in the more conspicuous people of the locality and studied their ways: the pretender to the throne of France, the monks of the nearby monastery, the director of a particular factory, two rather unconventional village priests. He learned to distinguish between the mystery of the Mass and the imperfections of the Church which administered the sacrament. He was very sensitive to the beauty of nature and to the elemental beings in it. So his early life was rich, though unconventional. When looking back on his childhood Steiner remarked on the dichotomy of life around him: the peace, intimacy and beauty of the unspoiled landscape and the busy life of the railway with all the latest technical inventions and the industrial activities which it engendered. He was attracted by both. There was no comparable balance in him between the Church and modern scientific attitudes. His father was a freethinker – later, in his retirement he returned to the Church – and the son was neither confirmed nor continued with his religion lessons once he had reached the age of fourteen when these lessons ceased to be compulsory. By this time he had left the village school and went to the *Realschule* in the nearby town of Wiener Neustadt. The school provided secondary education with a modern bias. Classical languages were not taught – again, he had to make up for this loss when a tutor in Vienna – but he received an excellent grounding in mathematics and the sciences. For father was resolved that his gifted son ought to study and eventually become a railway engineer. This resolve meant a real sacrifice for the family who lost an additional breadwinner, a loss they could not easily afford.

Liberation through Geometry

It was the scientific subjects which fascinated Rudolf Steiner most. Every year his teachers published some scientific studies of their own and very soon Steiner had taught himself enough mathematics and physics to understand these rather advanced publications. During boring lessons he studied philosophical writings, particularly those of Kant. A friendly doctor opened his library to him and introduced him to the German classics. He learned bookbinding in order to bind his own textbooks. But probably the greatest gain of these school years came early, at about thirteen years. He suddenly realised that the rectangles and triangles about which the teacher spoke existed in the mind only. So it was possible to speak about the realm of the mind and speak about it with the utmost precision. He set himself the goal of speaking with equal precision about his own inner world and so being able to communicate to others the *totality* of his experience.

Vienna

Throughout the greater part of his twenties Steiner lived, first, close to, and later in Vienna. Suddenly he was exposed to a bewildering variety of new impressions, new relations and problems, political, social, spiritual and practical. He found himself in the capital of a multi-lingual empire beset by social problems and national dissensions. He attended parliamentary sessions and studied outstanding politicians. But he did not remain simply an observer, he felt that he had to make a definite commitment. A German-speaking Austrian of his generation had to decide whether to lay the greater stress on the German or the Austrian component of his cultural heritage. The Austrian: European, feudal, Roman Catholic, easy-going, fairly tolerant. The German: national, dynamic, Protestant, modern, efficient. We shall see later how highly Steiner valued the supra-national dimension of Austria. But for two good reasons he chose to identify with the German element. He had already formed a high opinion of German literature and philosophy, particularly of the time of Goethe, compared to which Austrian achievements seemed paltry. Equally, he admired modern efficiency. While still at school he rejoiced over the introduction of the metric system in Austria. The same respect for modern efficiency is conveyed in a letter describing his first impressions of Germany.[3] Quite unlike Austria, he observes,

Germany displays the character of a unified people. An earlier letter[4] gives us a brief insight into the political attitudes of the twenty-three year old. In other words, he advocates democracy and cultural freedom for all the peoples of Austria while feeling that German culture has some special achievements to offer. Typically for Steiner, he also wants the German speakers in Austria to work towards a new social order, not dominated by the power of money, and supportive of culture.

His immediate interest was, of course, directed to the Technical University and its life. Very soon he was up to his neck in student activities: editor of a liberal weekly, treasurer of a student society, member of a debating club, etc. His studies, however, took on an entirely unexpected turn. He felt a spiritual kinship to Prof. Schröer who represented the humanities in this technological environment. The professor was not used to such attention and soon there developed a mutual feeling of respect and friendship. Schröer reinforced Steiner's interest in, and love of Goethe, and soon realised that his young pupil was capable of undertaking a task which he himself had been meant to do, but for which he lacked the necessary capacities: the job of editing Goethe's scientific writings. This task was later to take Steiner from Vienna to Weimar where the Duchess of this little state had sponsored the 'definitive' edition of Goethe's complete works. But first, the young man had time and leisure to explore the cultural landscape of Vienna.

A Widened Environment

The last six years of his time in Vienna Steiner spent in the house of Pauline and Ladislaus Specht, a cotton merchant. He had to look after the four Specht boys. With three of them this meant looking after their homework and generally widening their horizon. But Otto, the third son, could at the age of ten hardly read and write, was unable to face any intellectual strain and was also unusual in his behaviour. The success which Steiner had in this boy's education is probably the earliest testimony to his amazing achievement in many and diverse fields. The backward boy was later able to go to grammar school and eventually to study medicine. He died as a doctor in the First World War.

The Spechts treated Steiner as a member of their family. For the first time he no longer felt the burden of poverty. He lived in a highly cultured, well-to-do family who opened up to him an entirely new level of society in their comfortable flat in Vienna and their country house at one of Austria's loveliest lakes. But he had also plenty of time for himself, both for his work and for establishing new relationships. In the house of the young writer Marie Eugenie delle Grazie he met writers and university professors, some with an intimate knowledge of Roman Catholicism. They stimulated his philosophical interests and gave him an insight into certain spiritual traditions of the Church. He came in touch with some of the first theosophists in Vienna. He took a certain interest in their literature, but was not pleased by the unscientific nature of their conversation. However, he developed a strong connection with Rosa Mayreder, a member of Vienna's cultural elite, author of the libretto of Hugo Wolf's only opera and one of the first feminists. There was a mutual understanding between them in social matters and questions of individual morality. In those years were formed the thoughts which Steiner was later to put forward in his *Philosophy of Freedom*, and he found nobody with whom he could better discuss them than this outstanding and progressive woman.

Three Encounters

The years in Vienna widened Steiner's horizon immensely. They also deepened his inner experience. Already at the beginning of his university studies he met two men of whose importance for his inner development he has given us some indications. The information concerning the first of these was sufficient for Emil Bock, a quarter of a century after Steiner's death, to identify the man described and to interview one of his sons, as well as a few other elderly people who remembered him from their youth.[5] His name was Felix Koguzki. He was a herbalist and a rather poor man. He had an extensive knowledge of herbal lore, and was the owner of a library of books on mystical and occult subjects. He was a man of high morality, spiritual profundity and an instinctive awareness of the virtues of plants. "There were a lot of immense occult depths in this man", Steiner stated later.[6] The two had many conversations and through Felix Steiner learned that there existed a vast store of traditional wisdom which was soon to disappear completely from the folk culture of Central Europe. Felix was the first man among Steiner's acquaintances who like him appreciated the moral and spiritual dimensions of nature and so the conversations with Felix must have been most precious to Steiner.

An even more important meeting followed, but this time Steiner's indications were purposely so general that the man has never been traced. Steiner met his Master, – the man who sought him out and taught him how to train his innate spiritual gifts so that they could be increased, disciplined and refined, and become the conscious tool of a personality of the highest moral responsibility and intellectual capacity. The French writer Edouard Schuré was one of the very few, possibly the only man, to whom Steiner revealed more about this master. In the preface to the French edition of *Christianity as a Mystical Fact* Schuré describes this master as a man of unusual dynamism and states that he had charged Steiner to become an out-and-out materialist as the only way of overcoming materialism in the end.[7]

Of all this none of Steiner's Viennese friends had any idea. But there was one man, Friedrich Eckstein, who mediated between the two worlds in which Steiner lived, the cultural circles of Vienna and the inner world of Felix and the Master. Eckstein was one of the most knowledgeable men of his age. A chemist and industrialist, music lover and close friend of Anton Bruckner, alpinist and traveller, he also had a profound knowledge of traditional occultism. To him Steiner could go if he wanted any academic exposition of occult facts. Steiner was in complete harmony with Goethe's way of looking at nature, but it was Eckstein who could explain to him the symbolism and occult terminology in the poet's writings. Eckstein outlived Rudolf Steiner. But it is clear from his autobiography[8] that Rudolf Steiner never unveiled to him the insights which he had gained by now.

Looking back at the ten years in Vienna we can isolate three different spheres of experience in Steiner's life. There was his normal social life in which he met an extraordinary variety of people: poor students, rich merchants, Cistercian monks, feminists, writers, university professors, socialists, philosophers. There was his inner life, now consciously taken in hand, deepened and widened. The only outward signs of it are his scientific and philosophical writings and his occupation with the thoughts which were to form his *Philosophy of Freedom*. A third layer of experience was his discovery of a number of historical strands which presuppose, not necessarily the same stage of consciousness as his own, but related stages which gave expression to the perceived relationship of the world of the senses *and* the world of the spirit: Theosophists, Cistercians, Goetheanists, Felix and his traditional folklore, and also some impressive representatives of idealistic philosophy.

Weimar

The seven years from 1890 to 1897 Steiner lived in Weimar, one of a number of scholars editing Goethe's complete works. This academic enterprise was financed by the ducal court and the Duke and Duchess came occasionally to be informed about the progress of the work. The staff consisted of German scholars and there was a constant stream of interested people from other parts of the world. But the social environment was stuffy in the extreme and parochial in comparison with Vienna. In Weimar, – this town of "classical mummies"[9] – he found hardly anybody to talk to. The complaint was voiced repeatedly in the letters. He felt an exile from Vienna. Now he was living "on the tombs of German greatness".[10] Nobody spoke as an individual, but only according to his place in the social hierarchy. Steiner was disgusted by the way people, the staff of the Goethe Institute included, kow-towed to the Duke. He himself treated the Duke as he treated anybody else. He addressed him in the proper fashion but "I did not change my self-opinionated manner which people have so often complained about".[11]

In Weimar Steiner came in touch with two contemporaries whose work and destiny continued to occupy him over many years: Ernst Haeckel and Friedrich Nietzsche. The former was a popular protagonist of Darwinism, the latter stood for a new morality, far removed from traditional Christianity and conventional forms of behaviour. Steiner sided with both these men, though he realised their limitations as well. The important factor for him was that they challenged hallowed attitudes and opened up new areas for thought and investigation.

Berlin

In Weimar Steiner lived in the house of a widow, Anna Eunike, who had two adolescent children. He took an increasing responsibility for the welfare of these two and when in 1897 he went to Berlin Frau Eunike followed him with son and daughter. Soon after this removal

Steiner and Frau Eunike married. There exists at least one description of the way the couple behaved towards each other. Alwin Rudolph – about whom we shall hear later, – tells us of their puzzling relationship, too familiar for a boarder and landlady, too distant for man and wife. They separated after some time and in 1911 she died. One of her two children is known to have always spoken with the greatest affection for the man who for some time had been their stepfather.

Steiner had gone to Berlin because he had been able to acquire a weekly, the *Magazin für Literatur* "in order to have a forum where I could express to the world ideas which I considered truly contemporary".[12] However, it turned out to be the wrong forum. Many subscribers belonged to the academic establishment and were outraged when they realised that this new editor was a man of radical leanings who had exchanged letters with John Henry Mackay on 'Individual Anarchism' and spoken up for Zola and Dreyfus. The more progressive portion of the subscribers was not large enough to support the *Magazin* and after hardly more than three years Steiner had to retire. But through the literary and theatrical activities of these progressive readers a new stratum of society opened up for Steiner, the literary Berlin of the turn of the century. English-speaking readers will be largely unfamiliar with its writers, with the exception of August Strindberg and Frank Wedekind. But they were a most interesting assortment of people and almost as forceful and radical as their successors of the 1920s.

Then a second forum became available to Steiner. He was offered the post of a lecturer at a Workers' College and kept this post for seven years. We have two descriptions of the impression which the personality of Rudolf Steiner, the style of his lectures and their content made on on students, – who almost universally came from the Socialist Workers' Movement. One report is by Johanna Muecke who later followed Steiner into the anthroposophical movement, the other by Alwin Rudolph who was unable to make this step. For this reason his report, written many years later, is particularly valuable.[13] It describes Steiner's impact on the Berlin workmen who appreciated his commitment to his subject, his example and his totally undogmatic approach. However, there were difficulties. The organisers of the classes belonged to the Party apparatus and had increasing doubts about Steiner's reliability. Eventually, they forced a vote at a meeting of Steiner's students who voted 348 to 12 in favour of their lecturer.

Nevertheless, he was dismissed. So Steiner had lost his audience among the working class as well as among the middle classes.

It was in these years in Berlin that Steiner had an overwhelming experience of the reality of Christ, an experience which we shall mention again. (See Chapter Five.) Although it changed his whole existence it is very doubtful whether anything of it transpired to his friends at this time. What he now had to say was infinitely more than what most of the readers of the *Magazin* or his audience in the evening classes wanted to hear. But he took no steps to find a new audience or to cry, prophetlike, in the wilderness. In 1899 nobody could possibly have forecast the direction in which he, as a matter of fact, was to go.

The Berlin Theosophists

In 1900 Steiner received an invitation to give a lecture to a small group of people who met at the house of Count and Countess Brockdorff-Rantzau, members of the German-Danish aristocracy. They were theosophists and Steiner chose for his subject *Goethe's Secret Revelation*. The success of this lecture was so great that he was asked to give, first, one and then a second series of weekly lectures, in 1900/1 and 1901/2 respectively. These lectures were later issued in book form. Typically for the new Steiner, they dealt with spiritual matters and were centred on Christianity.[14]

This stage in Steiner's activity deserves a closer look. He had met theosophists in Vienna, but had not taken to them. He reacted negatively to theosophists he encountered at the court in Weimar. Once again "I immersed myself in the mystical element in which I had swum in Vienna for some time, to an almost frightening degree . . . One might welcome this phenomenon (i.e. Theosophy at the ducal court) as it probably is the last stage before the final demise."[15] That Steiner now accepted the invitation to lecture to theosophists shows on the one hand the effect of his Damascus experience and on the other his lifelong conviction: that the important thing is not people's beliefs, but who they themselves are. He met in this circle a number of people who responded deeply to his central concern which so far he had been unable to communicate to anybody. The foremost of his students was Marija von Sivers, the daughter of a Russian Admiral. She approached Steiner with the question: "Is it not possible to establish a spiritual teaching as profound as that of the East, but firmly based on European and Christian foundations?" This direct challenge enabled Steiner to speak about his inner world. A human need had been expressed to which he answered gladly and in fullest measure. The Brockdorff-Rantzaus were also greatly impressed. They felt they had found a spiritual teacher who could rally and invigorate theosophists in Germany. So they approached Mrs Besant in London with the suggestion of founding a Theosophical Society in Germany and making Rudolf Steiner its general secretary. This demanded not a little generosity on the part of Mrs Besant and her advisors. Rudolf Steiner was not a member of the Theosophical Society and his approach was widely different from that of English-speaking theosophists who were basing themselves more and more on Indian tradition.

So Rudolf Steiner went to London to discuss matters with the leading theosophists there. How loyal he remained to his former connections and how open he was to whatever the future might hold for him can be gleaned from the following two incidents. Before setting out for London he applied for the job of literary editor of Vienna's most important newspaper. It was his wish to test fully the opportunities which life might grant him and to allow his work to develop regardless of his own wishes and ambitions. On the way back he stopped in Paris and sent a postcard to one of his students in the workers' evening classes: "I should like to send you my sincere greetings from *this* spot."[16] The spot was the Place de la Bastille.

Had Rudolf Steiner found at last his right forum in the Theosophical Society after the *Magazin* and the evening classes had proved unsatisfactory? Looking back many years later at this period in his life he described these theosophists – many of whom were later to form the Anthroposophical Society – as 'homeless souls', people who did not feel at home in the culture of the day. They felt that the churches could not face satisfactorily the new problems which science and a rapidly changing society posed. Nor could they accept the smug complacency and hidebound optimism of materialism. But many of them – not all – felt quite comfortable and at home in the cosy bourgeois society of pre-war days. They were people whose formative years had been spent in the German equivalent of the Victorian era and were without sympathy for, or even an understanding of Steiner's social concerns. He had to wait longer until fully 'homeless souls' came to him. Before the War a group of Russians flocked to him, many of them artists, who had opted out of their rather comfortable lives in tension-ridden Russia, and were fairly amused by the satiety and complacency of the German bourgeoisie among whom they were now living as alienated exiles. After the War young Central Europeans gathered round Steiner. They felt defeated, disillusioned and betrayed and were looking for an entirely new way of life. Until this time was to arrive Steiner had to confine himself to what was possible for the audience which had gathered around him. But we shall look first at what was not possible.

Disappointments

He could not interest them in the moral individualism of his *Philosophy of Freedom*. Only as late as 1918 did he feel confident enough to bring out the second edition of this work. Nor could he interest them in his social concerns although he tried. The way his endeavours were received forced Steiner to drop this subject for many years. The greatest disappointment came, however, right at the beginning of the German Section of the Theosophical Society.

Near the end of his life Steiner explained that his most important concern had been the communication of the results of his investigations into Karma. In another chapter we shall look more closely at this complex realm. (See Chapter Five.) For the moment it must suffice to say that while Steiner continued to use the Indian term he gave it a totally new meaning and put it into a Western and Christian context. He chose deliberately the realm of Karma with which he was so intimately linked as the theme of the course with which he wanted to inaugurate the work of the newly formed group. He called the course *Practical Karma Exercises*. Though there exist no transcripts of this course Steiner's intentions are perfectly clear. He did not want to teach, to state, to reveal. He wanted to widen the inner sensitivities of the people who formed his third 'forum', to awaken them to open up to themselves the hidden depths of their past existence and the cosmic forces which helped them in their incarnation process. The result was shattering and disappointing. The attempt had to be abandoned. "Thus it was quite impossible to continue the programme, and the Theosophical movement in Germany took on a more theoretical character", he said twenty years later.[17]

To the present writer this seems a momentous shift in Steiner's attitude to his newly-won audience. His intention had been to rouse them, to awaken in them an awareness of their own spiritual dimension. In a letter[18] he emphasises his intention of of becoming an *awakener* of men. It makes quite clear what he had in mind when he wanted to begin his work in the German Section of the Theosophical Society with practical karma exercises. He writes:"I shall rely on the power which enables me to set 'spiritual disciples' on the path of development". This aim was not abandoned, but henceforth it was achieved indirectly. In the foreground stood a spiritual teaching enunciated by a spiritual teacher. He who could read between the lines, become sensitive to the implications and undertones of the teacher's word, could learn to re-orientate himself socially, morally and religiously. He could also approach the teacher and ask for guidance for his personal development. For the others what Steiner seemed to give was a teaching, that means, something that was accepted at the teacher's authority, however strongly and frequently this particular teacher pleaded for independent judgement and personal experience. Steiner remained the teacher of freedom. It was not for him to lay down the law as to what his pupils were to make of his words. This lay in their own discretion.

When in 1911 Rudolf Steiner tried, within this teaching, to give concrete examples of karma connections, he again met with incomprehension and the attempt was not repeated until 1924, by which time the social composition of his audience and their spiritual needs and expectations had vastly changed.

An Independent Teacher

There are a number of documents which emphasise Steiner's intentions in 1902. In becoming a teacher to an integral part of the Theosophical Society it was essential for him to keep his independence. This was granted. At the same time he wrote to a German theosophist: "The best thing, without any doubt, would be something entirely new without reliance on what exists already. But I believe that *perhaps* we shall be able to achieve the best also within the framework of the Theosophical Society . . . I clearly see the risk to which I am exposing myself, and I believe I have to expose myself to it."[19] So it hardly seems exaggerated when in retrospect Steiner says: "I have never tried to establish contact with the Theosophical Society, but rather paradoxically as it may seem, the Theosophical Society tried establishing contact with me . . . At this time I had not read any books of the Theosophical Society – I always had a certain horror of them – and" only now began "to read these things in my official capacity as it were."[20]

Increasing Activity

Together with Marie von Sivers, as she was called in Germany, Steiner began to build up the organisation of the German Section of the Theosophical Society and to give it a spiritual content of its own. Marie von Sivers had asked the decisive question and Steiner in turn decided to go forward with the Theosophical Society only after he had been assured of her support and co-operation. She, a powerful and highly gifted woman, was from now on his inseparable companion who participated in every aspect of his life and work. They formalised this relationship only after the outbreak of the War and so the Russian Marija von Sivers became the Austrian Marie Steiner.

The spiritual teaching came in the form of lectures and books, and through a periodical called *Lucifer-Gnosis*. Steiner remained based in Berlin and there most of his early public lectures were given. He spoke more intimately to members of the Society. Groups – called *Zweige* (branches) – sprang up in many German towns, the most important apart from Berlin being Munich and Stuttgart in the south of the country. So a great deal of travelling had to be undertaken and soon it was found that members of the Society were best served by a whole series of lectures on a single theme, the so-called *Zyklen* (lecture courses). As Steiner usually chose a new subject for each series there were always a number of members who followed him from place to place to share in the experience of hearing him speak and to assimilate the ever-widening content of these lectures. Soon requests for lectures came also from other European countries and by 1914, when war broke out, Steiner had held lectures in an area bounded by London, Bergen, Uppsala, Helsinki, Prague, Budapest, Palermo and Paris.

In these years were written three books which come nearest to being introductions to Anthroposophy, *Theosophy, Occult Science* and *Knowledge of the Higher Worlds*.[21] *Theosophy* deals mainly with man as a physical-spiritual entity, and his roots in a spiritually perceived universe. *Occult Science* goes partly over the same ground, but speaks of processes and developments. It describes the very gradual growth of man out of cosmic forces, his equally gradual isolation from these forces and the establishment of earthly individualities often unaware of their spiritual origin. *Knowledge of the Higher Worlds* gives a detailed and intimate description of modern man's path of development in order to regain and deepen his awareness of his roots in the spirit. As mentioned in the previous page, this book had its origin in a series of articles in the magazine which Steiner edited. This magazine flourished for a few years until Steiner's workload made its further publication impossible.

When Rudolf Steiner had first lectured to the theosophists assembled at the Brockdorffs' house he addressed them as any lecturer would address an educated audience of laymen, if we may judge by the printed versions of these lectures. (See *The Berlin Theosophists*.) When he became the official leader of the German theosophical movement he adopted at first a number of terms from Indian and Anglo-American Theosophy. But gradually he created his own vocabulary and even where he retained the older terms, e.g. *karma*, he imbued them with new life and meaning. Soon Steiner found that there were members of the Society who yearned for an intensification of their inner life and he established for these an Esoteric School. This School was given oral esoteric instructions which culminated in formulas and verses for the pupil's private meditation. In 1906 Steiner founded a second form of esoteric teaching.

We have seen that by the time Steiner left Vienna he had contact with a number of traditional forms of esoteric teaching. (See *Three Encounters*.) It seems that he himself never made a move to contact them, but that life established such contacts quite naturally. We have also seen that he did not necessarily approve of what he met. (See *The Berlin Theosophists*.) But however radically new and modern his outlook, he felt it right to build links to the past so that the new could transform what was old and – possibly – dying. Now he was offered a chance to form a link with the Masonic tradition, and with his respect for the old wisdom and for the historically given he accepted this opening. In January 1906 he received permission from a certain Theodor Reuss to officiate within the Ordo Templi Orientis (O.T.O.). This caused certain difficulties later as Reuss' style of life caused wide-spread comment. Steiner, however, used this permission to build up a second school of esoteric teaching unconnected to his Esoteric School. Apart from instructions, the meetings of this circle "contained ritual acts in cultic form. Their purpose was to deepen supersensible insights, to intensify the participants' emotional being and to strengthen their will."[22] (Both esoteric circles were dissolved in

1914 and do not exist today.)

The content of Steiner's lecture cycles was soon widely disseminated. People took notes and reported what they had heard to their friends at home. Steiner did not disapprove of this development. He held that people should be encouraged to reproduce in their own words those experiences in his lectures which had meant most to them and with which they could identify. Of course, sometimes versions of Steiner's lectures circulated which were highly sensational and a distortion of what Steiner had said. Nevertheless, he could not bring himself to fix in cold print what had been for him an almost sacred act and for his audience a many-layered experience. (See Chapter Two.) Marie von Sivers thought otherwise. She was anxious to keep the teaching uncontaminated by personal misunderstandings and misrepresentations, and so invested a great amount of time and labour in bringing out cyclostyled versions of these lectures. Steiner did not stop her, but repeatedly made it clear that this had not happened on his initiative. Usually these copies bore the comment "Unrevised by the lecturer." Ideally, Steiner would have re-written all his lectures for publication and was occasionally able to do so. He was immensely grateful to Albert Steffen when the latter once retold and published an account of a course on education which Steiner had given at the request of a group of teachers from England and Wales.

Tensions

With the growth of Steiner's activities accelerating all over Europe his relations with the central figures of the Theosophical Society were bound to reach a critical stage. Indeed, the difficulties had been there from the start. They might have been faced consciously and possibly solved. Instead, they led to increasing tension and to a break. There were three reasons for this development.

One was the difficulty of standing between the two sides. In the Theosophical Society were many interesting people and, in particular, Annie Besant had stood out as an independent and progressive woman. To a large extent, they looked back to the occult revelations of their founder, H. P. Blavatsky, and partly they tried to find in India new sources of occult insight. Great play was made with messages which were supposed to emanate from certain hidden Masters. In Rudolf Steiner the leaders of the Theosophical Society found an entirely different attitude. From the beginning he had insisted on his independence; he could only speak about what he himself could vouch for. He spoke a different language and appealed to the power of thinking which for him was the key to independent spiritual investigation. Surely, in the long run only two courses were possible. If the theosophical establishment accepted the phenomenon of Steiner, they would have to make him the leader of the whole movement. If they did not accept his independent stance and claim of spiritual autonomy, they had to get rid of him as a perpetual irritant.

Looking at the documents of those days we are struck by the initial degree of tolerance and fairness on either side. A solution seemed possible given so much goodwill. But we must also not forget the political situation of the day. Anglo-German suspicions grew at an ever-increasing speed. To many Englishmen Steiner must have seemed a typical product of German push and ambition, while among some German theosophists the London establishment smacked of British imperialism. In such an atmosphere the solution became rapidly more difficult.

However, it was the third complex of questions which brought about the break. The more Steiner's teaching grew the more noticeable became his *essential* differences with established theosophy. In 1907 Steiner chaired an International Congress of Theosophists at Munich. There it became apparent that he did not only articulate a spiritual message: he also wanted to change the world. He had, in fact, started, however slightly and tentatively, to give the hall in which the congress met an appearance commensurate to the coming events. He had used art to make spiritual realities sense-perceptible. With the help of earthly substances he began to transform the environment. It was an endeavour alien to many theosophists, but one in which Steiner persisted. Indeed, year by year new realms were opened up for imaginative and creative activities out of spiritual insights. The intention was to establish an environment in which modern man could thrive as a social and spiritual being. Traditional theosophists sensed that Steiner had embarked on a path on which they were not prepared to accompany him: the regeneration of modern culture in all its widest aspects, artistic, social, scientific. Theosophy was to remain a movement concerned with the spiritual and moral being of man, with study, devotion and meditation. It was not concerned with the world at large.

But what troubled theosophists even more was the fact that

Steiner's teaching centred ever more strongly on what he called the Mystery of Golgotha. For Theosophy all religions were equal – although an outside observer might have no difficulty in detecting a pro-Indian bias. Steiner too appreciated the various religions as expressions of men's understanding of spiritual realities according to their different stages of consciousness. He treated the *history* of the Christian religion in exactly the same way. But with the Mystery of Golgotha something *objective* had happened: the incarnation, death and resurrection of the Logos, the Word, had changed the spiritual-physical condition of the earth and of all men, irrespective of their religious beliefs or lack of them. (See Chapter Five.)

The point of separation was reached through Annie Besant's announcement that Christ had re-incarnated in one of two young Indian brothers. This was unacceptable to Steiner who saw in such an announcement a total misunderstanding of the central event of the history of the planet. His protest in turn led to counter measures, and the separation of Steiner from the Theosophical movement became inevitable. On 2nd February, 1913 the Anthroposophical Society was founded. Steiner continued to keep his independence – and never became a member of it. The new society comprised the majority of members of the Theosophical Society in Central Europe and sizeable parts of its Scandinavian, Dutch and Russian branches. A number of British theosophists also chose to join.

A word, however, about the outstanding man who unconsciously was the centre of this conflict. One of the two Indian brothers soon died, and so it seemed obvious to theosophists that Christ had reincarnated in the other. He was brought up with great care and love, and Mrs Besant looked on him as her son. He was Krishnamurti, a man to whom anybody concerned with spiritual matters cannot but look up with deep respect. He was early burdened with the knowledge of his supposed identity to Christ. He had the greatness to renounce this pretention, knowing how much hurt and disappointment he had to inflict on the woman who had invested in him so much love and hope. All through his life he testified to his spiritual awareness. He only pointed to it knowing that any articulate pronouncements of spiritual realities are only too likely to turn spiritual life into dogma, and create churches and sects. Steiner, of course, went the opposite way. He articulated some of his spiritual insights and then strove to find social forms which would vitiate dogmatism and sectarianism. (See Chapter Nine.)

The Arts

In the years immediately before the outbreak of the War Rudolf
Steiner's activities expanded in new directions, and crystallised
around a new centre: Dornach near Basel in neutral Switzerland. The
outlines of his teaching stood out clearly in the published books and
the transcripts of his lecture courses, the number of his pupils was
growing, he had separated from the Theosophical Society. The seed
planted at the Munich Congress had begun to germinate and the
anthroposophical movement had started to develop an increasing
number of artistic activities. (See *Tensions*.) Plays by Edouard Schuré
were read and later performed, and in 1910 Steiner wrote his first
Mystery Play, which was followed by three others in three successive
years. He himself produced the plays giving indications and
suggestions about new approaches to the arts of speaking, acting,
moving, painting etc. The plays were performed in a commercial
theatre in Munich. This fact placed considerable constraints upon
performers and audience, and ran counter to one of Steiner's central
convictions, that there is in the world, and should be in human affairs
an identity between inner and outer reality. His Mystery Plays needed
a stage of their own and efforts were made to build a theatre in Munich
specially designed for this purpose. A design was made for a building
which presented to the world at large a modern frontage, while the
more striking architectural aspects were reserved for the interior of
the building.[23] However, the Munich authorities made difficulties
which could have delayed construction.

But then Steiner was offered a plot of land on the hill of Dornach,
which at this time was still a small peasant village, though it has now
grown into a suburb of Basel. Dornach seemed ideal because of the
liberal building by-laws of the Canton of Solothurn in which it lies.
Steiner visited the site and decided to accept the offer. Reports of
eye-witnesses make it probable that in the twenty-four hours prior to
this decision he had a series of shattering insights concerning the
specific nature and history of this landscape. They seemed to tax him
to the limit. The decision being taken, he never uttered any doubts.
Work was set in train; the foundation stone was laid on 20th
September 1913; and when within a year war broke out, the work,
though impeded, was able to be continued. Men and women of 17
nations, most of them at war with each other, worked on this building
within earshot of the rumbling of the guns on the Western Front.

The Goetheanum

It is difficult to give an idea of the immensity of the architectural undertaking without going into detail.[24] We need stress here only three aspects: the unusual design, the variety of the new techniques applied, and the interesting work-force which had assembled around Steiner. He had in mind a ground plan of two intersecting circles, the larger one forming the auditorium, the smaller one the stage. Each was crowned by a cupola. Steiner had himself to face the problem of how these cupolas were to intersect and mutually support each other. The whole structure was made of wood, largely handcarved, and the domes covered with silver-grey Norwegian slate. He had set himself and his co-workers exciting problems by working with new materials and treating old established materials in new ways. The ceiling of the cupola was to be painted in colours extracted from plants.

The result was a new technology. The windows were to be of coloured glass: but instead of using the medieval technique – a mosaic-like design of small pieces of glass – the Goetheanum windows consisted of large panes of one colour; different windows had different colours. These panes had to be sculpted by mechanical drills so that the light shining through varying thicknesses of glass should create pictorial forms. There were two types of forms, both deeply stirring. The windows and the paintings were illustrations of Steiner's insights into spiritual realities. Even in reproductions today they are arresting in their power, intensity and directness. They owe little or nothing to earlier traditions. Symbolism is almost totally absent.

The forms of the building itself were exercises in metamorphosis, examples of the gradual changes of organic forms. Where function was paramount, it was to be made manifest. The staircase was to invite the visitor upwards; the door declared how it was to be opened. A building arose which, through the demands it made, was exciting and challenging to all who worked on it.

Dornach

Three types of people were involved in the work: Swiss masons, carpenters, tilers who were employed on usual terms, Anthroposophists with technical or artistic skills, and unpaid volunteers who were overjoyed to work on a constructive task in the midst of the worst slaughter Europe had known. Steiner had been able to attract many men and women with considerable artistic gifts, who were now able to devote their skills to a huge co-operative effort. They and others less gifted, but equally anxious to serve Steiner's work, found in Dornach a new home. Here they could live close to the man they respected and begin to live with a new life style. They practised the new art of eurythmy which Steiner had begun to evolve. They acted in scenes from his plays and from Goethe's Faust. They found creative sources in themselves of which they had so far been unaware. They had to find new homes. Often they had meals together in the canteen near the building site, they made music together, they went to the lectures which Steiner regularly gave. They made Steiner's intentions a reality, – but they also caused him many problems. He was plagued by trivial requests for advice; he was deeply disturbed by occasional outbursts of parochialism, nationalism and destructive jealousy. This was not surprising. He lived in the midst of an inward-looking community, which contained within it strong tensions between nationalities and between different life-styles, – the wealthy bourgeois and the classless artist – tensions which only he could resolve.

Facing the Imminent Chaos

But Steiner himself was not enclosed in this inward-looking community. His mind was much concerned with the war that was shaking Europe to its foundations. From the beginning he had endeavoured to make his audiences aware of the tragedies being enacted, of the young and promising lives being sacrificed, of the pain of the bereaved, of the anxieties felt everywhere. He tried to strengthen and enlighten the people whom he addressed. He never failed to begin his lectures with a meditation for those in danger, and one for those who had already gone through death. However, late in 1916 he adopted a different attitude: that of the warning prophet. It was the time when the two Central European powers, and Austria in particular, sent out clear signals that they were ready for a negotiated peace. Steiner realised that this was Europe's last chance. If these peace offers were spurned, Europe would be thrown into chaos and destruction. They were spurned.[25] Steiner's response was to think ahead. Was there a way in which chaos could be averted? What new social forms were fit for the new Europe?

He spoke his mind to the few hundred anthroposophists working at Dornach. Many of these must have been bewildered and shocked. They had flocked to Steiner in search of spiritual insights, in the hope of comfort and guidance, and now were told of problems which they had always tried to evade, of possible solutions which seemed more dangerous to established habits than Marxism.

Nevertheless, during the next few years Steiner gave a great part of his time to writing and lecturing about social questions and to talking with businessmen and politicians, workers and industrialists. We shall look at these endeavours in some detail in the chapter on Social Renewal, but want to stress already now that Steiner's social ideas are no arbitrary adjunct, but a necessary corollary to his teachings on spiritual matters. In spite of his intense commitment Steiner's social intentions failed to kindle a sufficient number of people and he himself abandoned the effort in 1921.

But at the same time an entirely new kind of person was attracted to him: young men who had fought in the War became totally disillusioned with the values of pre-war society, and saw in Steiner a man who would show them the way to build up a new and modern life out of the ruins of the old. Their initiatives opened up new possibilities for Steiner's activity, which somewhat curtailed, but never impaired his established activities, – working at the Goetheanum building, giving lectures at Dornach and travelling to the extent that war and post-war conditions allowed.

The Waldorfschule

In one respect, however, Steiner's efforts towards social renewal had lasting results. At the Waldorf-Astoria cigarette factory a worker had said to Steiner: "I see what you are aiming at. But for us it is too late. Could you not do something to give our children a truly human education?"[26] And so with the financial support of Emil Molt, the owner of the factory, the *Waldorfschule* was founded. The impulse behind it was social. The school became a source of immense joy to Steiner, who spent much time visiting classes and discussing with teachers all the issues with which the new venture had to deal.[27] Today there exist about 400 such schools in Europe, the English-speaking world and South America. In the Netherlands and Germany they are to be found in practically every large or medium-sized town.

The years from 1920 to 1922 were a difficult time for Steiner, but in many ways a rewarding one as well. The difficulties were caused by the failure of his social ideas and the increasing tension between the older anthroposophists, – often harking back to the relatively untroubled pre-war days, – and the newcomers, impatient and dynamic activists. They came to Steiner with ever new requests. Sometimes they found older members who wanted to work with them, sometimes they were totally alone. There were new schools to be founded, laboratories opened, work with handicapped children begun. Young doctors and medical students gathered around him and Dr Ita Wegman. Actors wanted to learn from him and Marie Steiner. New international connections were started and old ones taken up again. In Britain much interest was shown in Steiner's new art of education, particularly by Prof. Mackenzie of Cardiff University and by Margaret Macmillan. Steiner visited Britain in 1922, 1923 and 1924, and each time gave a course on education. In addition, he spoke to Anthroposophists and gave introductory courses.

The Christian Community

A very interesting suggestion was put to him soon after the War: Would he found a new church? A group of young theologians had experienced the reality of Christ's activity, but the existing churches seemed to them fossilised. Steiner had always insisted that he did not see his role as the founder of a new religion. He was speaking about concrete spiritual realities, which would deepen the religious sensitivities of those who wished to take these facts into their meditative and contemplative life. Thereby they would also learn to understand more intimately the religion into which they were born or acquire a new religious awareness, outside any church. On the other hand, he always fully respected people's initiatives and helped where he could.

He put these young people in touch with Dr Rittelmeyer, a prominent German theologian and offered his *help* for the establishment of a new Christian ritual. Thus the *Christian Community* was founded and Friedrich Rittelmeyer became its first head. Typically for Steiner as well as the new movement, already the first group of priests consisted of women as well as men. Steiner took a close interest in the fortunes of the new church. But he also made it clear that this was not the religious department of the

Anthroposophical Society. He re-iterated more than once that the path which he recommended started with the contemplation of facts, spiritual and natural, and that this study would lead to increased religious awareness. Whether it would then find expression through participation in an established religion, and if so, in which religion, was a matter of individual decision.

Catastrophe

On the last night of 1922 the great wooden building of the Goetheanum was burned to the ground. Ten years of effort and sacrifice were destroyed by an act of arson. The members of the Society were stunned and horrified. Steiner had repeatedly hinted that the building would not stand long and only recently had been warned of its imminent destruction. (See Chapter Two.) But when the blow fell his suffering was at least as deep and real as that of his helpers and friends. With incredible strength and courage he continued with his lectures as arranged.

Soon it was clear that a second Goetheanum would be built. True to his creative nature and to his sensitivity for the age in which he lived, the new building was to be no copy of the old. It was radically different in material and in design, – one of the very first large-scale structures in pre-stressed concrete. However, he felt he could not go forward without first clearing up the problem of the past. Had the body of Anthroposophists shown some spiritual strength and cohesion, the disaster might have been avoided. His first task, then, was the rebuilding of the Society.

In February he met delegates of the Anthroposophical Society in Germany, the largest part of the movement. He wanted to find suggestions which he could utilise in bringing new life and new forms into the Society. He found none, only discord. His followers seemed unable to deal constructively with the situation. Steiner therefore decided to act, having waited until the last possible moment. Let the young generation have their own Society, the *Free Anthroposophical Society*. Let each member ask himself where he wanted to belong, to the established society, the Free Society, or to both. His followers were horrified. Neither young nor old were happy with a solution that meant a split society. But for Steiner the principle of the freedom of the individual was paramount. No majority had the right to co-erce a minority.

During the next months Steiner visited as many European countries as possible. He founded or re-founded a number of national societies, the Anthroposophical Society in Great Britain among them. He then invited members to meet at Christmas in Dornach with a view to founding a new society containing within itself these national societies. But for a long time he was unsure how to proceed. Too little had emerged from the membership at large. It seems that the decisive word was spoken as late as November 1923. It came from Ita Wegman, the medical doctor with whom Steiner had of late been working increasingly closely.

The Anthroposophical Society

What Rudolf Steiner had to say at Christmas 1923 will be discussed at greater length in Chapter Nine. But a number of features impressed themselves most strongly on the participants of this conference. They felt a new beginning. A spring had descended on them holding the greatest promise. Steiner had himself founded the new society, – he who had so far had no responsibility for the Anthroposophical Society, but only for the teaching within it. He had founded this society, the General Anthroposophical Society, with the help of three women and two men who formed its *Vorstand*, its leadership.

The response of members was strong. Some, though, were anxious that the new activities might be too ambitious and demand more spiritual substance than some of its representatives could muster. But others felt that their deepest longings had been answered. From all quarters came new requests for help, and Steiner tried to answer them all. He travelled much. Teachers, doctors, farmers, priests and actors were all given new material for their work. During the greater part of September 1924 he gave five concurrent courses a day.

The Final Phase

Also, his own initiatives had changed. All his life he had wanted to speak about karma: not in vague or moralising terms, but through the minute observation of concrete facts. More than once he had embarked on such a venture, and every time he was forced to withdraw. This time he succeeded. The seven volumes of his *Karma Lectures* which he gave during 1924 open to the Anthroposophist an entirely new field of study. Also the tone of his lectures had changed.

In his earlier years he had used some of the vocabulary of the Theosophists, then he had created his own specific terms. Now he spoke in a new way: putting the facts of spiritual existence intimately before his hearers and giving them a feel for the esoteric life of the School he was establishing, a life which was to permeate every aspect of anthroposophical work and of the General Anthroposophical Society.

In the second half of September 1924 Steiner fell ill. His lectures had to be cancelled, – something which had never happened before. He made a heroic attempt to address members at Michaelmas, but had to break off before the lecture had reached its conclusion. He lived for another half-year, unable to leave his bed. His strength had suddenly drained away, he was completely exhausted. He felt he could have continued to carry his enormous work load – for considerable periods he slept hardly more than one hour a night – but the fact that Anthroposophists tried constantly to involve him in their private affairs, sometimes in a rather petty manner, was too much. He had never learned to refuse requests for help. In these last six months he also communicated with members in writing. He wrote weekly open letters which dealt with new aspects of his spiritual search, and also the greater part of his autobiography.[28]

He died on 30th March 1925. His death at the age of 64 came too soon for his friends and disciples. It was also a grievous blow to the new Society, which had not had time to find adequate working forms. The School existed only in a first stage. It was uncertain whether his successors would be able to work in harmony with each other. The situation in Europe looked bleak. Already German right-wing nationalists had tried, in Munich, to assassinate Steiner. He had indicated that an age of barbarism would descend on Europe in 1933. With such prospects for his movement, for Europe and for the world, the last half year must have been a bitter trial for a man of Steiner's activity and creative power.

Chapter Two
A Portrait of Rudolf Steiner

To speak about the character of a person is not to say anything about
the truth or otherwise of his convictions or teaching. Nevertheless, it
is legitimate to ask: what kind of a man was Rudolf Steiner?

This question, however, is not at all easy to answer. We can, and
shall give plenty of instances of his attitude and behaviour[1]; what we
lack are other people different from, but at the same time comparable
to him. He displays a universality of knowledge and a strength of
intellect which makes us think of Plato and Aristotle: but neither
possessed Steiner's practical knowledge – "a matter for slaves" – nor
his intimate spirituality, at least, judging by the extant literature. And
certainly he cannot be compared to an Eastern guru, and this for two
reasons: he lived *in* the world, suffering and shaping it, emotionally
involved with its fate and with the burdens and joys of his fellow men.
Also, he did not want to inspire belief. He wanted to be taken
seriously, but also to be closely scrutinised and even corrected.
Essentially, he was an awakener of human beings, a liberator. Very
rarely did he speak about himself and his motivation, but after his
death the following poem was discovered in one of his late notebooks:

> Ich möchte jeden Menschen
> Aus des Kosmos' Geist entzuenden,
> Daß er Flamme werde
> Und feurig seines Wesens
> Wesen entfalte.
>
> Die Andern, sie möchten
> Aus des Kosmos' Wasser nehmen,
> Was die Flammen verlösche
> Und wässrig alles Wesen
> Im Innern lähmt.
>
> O Freude, wenn die Menschenflamme
> Lodert auch da, wo sie ruht.
> O Bitternis, wenn das Menschending
> Gebunden wird da, wo es regsam sein möchte.[2]

These lines were rendered by Owen Barfield in English:

> Fain would I from the Spirit of the World
> Borrow wherewith to kindle Everyman,
> So that each one, himself a flame, unfold
> The Being of his being.
>
> Let others seek to draw from the World-water
> The wherewithal to quench those flames,
> To paralyse, to drown as from within
> All things that are.
>
> O joy, to see the flame that is Mankind
> Flare in the very niche where it abides.
> O gall, to see the thing that is mankind
> Bound, when it might leap up alert and free.

A Learner

Perhaps the most surprising feature of Steiner is his tenacity and ability to learn. He had to work hard to acquire earthly skills. At the age of ten he had a small vocabulary, found grammar and spelling irksome and experienced difficulties in relating to "the completely dry physical life".[3] After his removal to Weimar he wrote a letter to the Spechts thanking them for their hospitality and friendship. In it he referred to himself in his early twenties as the *unerfahrenen Büchermenschen*,[4] this inexperienced man whose only interest were books. Yet this is the same man who learned to sew on his buttons and heel his shoes, the man who proved an excellent administrator and negotiator. Herr Estermann, who for many years was in charge of the Goetheanum building, told the present writer about Steiner's architectural sketches: the first of each series could have been bettered by many a schoolboy, the fifth could not be improved on by the most gifted architect.

Assya Turgeneva who worked at the first Goetheanum describes Steiner as a woodcarver: "Next day when we stood with our tools before our work we were amazed about Dr Steiner's stamina. We had to make breaks after each half hour and our fingers were sore. The result of our work was as if a mouse had nibbled at the wood. But he stood for hours on his wooden box plying his chisel calmly and rhythmically, and quickly looking now and then on the little model of the work. As if in conversation with the wood or as if listening to the process, completely immersed in his work he stood and the form was released more and more out of the wooden block."[5]

Equally astonishing is his change in social manners. Gabriele Reuter, a German author, described him in his Weimar days. He "was radical and did not mince his words. One day he said in amazement that one of his acquaintances had not greeted him. 'Well, what have you done this time,' asked Frau Olden, whereupon he harmlessly answered in his Austrian intonation: 'I only called him a scum – and surely this is what he really is.' " Not so many years later he was a model of tolerance and courtesy.

Richard Specht – of whom more later – reported that Steiner in his twenties "was not a very moderately gifted draughtsman, but rather an immoderately ungifted one", and contrasted his artistic interests with his lack of artistic abilities. Yet thirty years later Steiner designed and partly painted the cupolas of the first Goetheanum. From the reproductions of his sketches these creations appear overpowering works of the imagination in a most modern manner, in their impact and subject matter reminiscent of Blake. A short time previously he had had to undertake the calculations for the construction of the two intersecting cupolas, as none of the architects of the Goetheanum was able to solve the mathematical difficulties inherent in this problem.

Ernst Lehrs tells of an architect who had known Steiner as the editor of the *Magazin*. Although not interested in Steiner's teachings he used an opportunity to visit the first Goetheanum. Its style seemed strange to him, but he was full of admiration for the organisational ability necessary for the erection of such a large-scale building. How could the man whom he had known as an editor acquire such capacities in so short a time?[6]

Discipline

Such work as well as the acquisition of the necessary skills was possible only through the iron discipline which he imposed on himself. He did with a minimum of sleep. In the last year of his life he spent a fortnight in Silesia where he gave his *Agricultural Course*. After a heavy day's work he sat down to a common meal, a leisurely and social affair. Later he went to his room where he attended to his large correspondence. Early in the morning a young man collected the letters and took them by motorcycle to the local post office. He calculated that Steiner had no more than one hour's sleep every day.[7] This extraordinary grip of a man in his sixties over the requirements of his body contrasts with his letters from Weimar. There are references to periods of tiredness, of slight depressions, of diminished good health. Later, Andrei Bely describes a whole series of incidents characteristic of Steiner's ability to cope with his tiredness[8] while another author described a particularly strenuous day followed by a car drive at night. "We arrived at Dornach at 3am. We had a meal at Rudolf Steiner's house. Deadly tired I dragged myself to the guesthouse where I stayed in those days. Steiner, however, who had behind him a particularly strenuous time in Stuttgart and had spent the last three nights without any sleep sat down at his desk and wrote an article for the magazine *Das Goetheanum*. This article had to go to print early in the morning."[9] If we visualise the incredible effort needed for such an achievement; if further we realise that this did not happen once, but frequently; and if we then compare this with his condition in the Weimar years we may well have reason to conclude that we are confronted with a man consciously and quietly harnessing spiritual forces for the mastery of his earthly tasks.

His discipline showed itself in other ways as well.[10] Wherever possible, he preferred to rely on himself. The young Herr Poeppig was not allowed to carry a pile of books for the sixty-year old Steiner.[11] Leinhas described how Steiner arrived at the railway station. He was early and carried his papers and his baggage. Again, the younger man was not allowed to help with the heavy leather case fastened with a belt.[12] After Steiner's death the local tax collector recounted how Steiner came in person to his office to pay his tax. Every year he appeared there punctually on the right day and always had the cash ready so that no change was required.[13] The same meticulous care which he bestowed on his practical responsibilities was also shown in his use of words and in his spiritual observations. Bely records[14] that in 1923, when bidding him farewell, Steiner for the first time omitted the familiar *Auf Wiedersehen* (see you again). He could do nothing else. For they were never to meet again. Rittelmeyer speaks of the death of a certain anthroposophist. Dr Steiner had advised the man's wife to take up eagerly any suggestion of an operation which her doctors might make. "If I see rightly there is something at the pyloric end of the stomach." The doctors thought otherwise and the man died. Steiner suggested a post-mortem "in order also to check my own observation."[15] Another time he said to Rittelmeyer: "I would not mind getting a touch of influenza in order to study it." The next day he had his influenza and he had it badly. But a few years later he was able to help Rittelmeyer when he in turn was suffering from a bout of it.[16]

A Lover of Men

Disciplined, austere and self-reliant he was, but towards others there was nothing of a puritan. He was open, understanding, tolerant and overflowing with love and gentle humour. Rittelmeyer describing his first personal meeting with Steiner emphasises the latter's "selfless surrender" to the total physical-spiritual being of his visitor.

"Upstairs, Rudolf Steiner was standing in the half-opened door through which another visitor had just passed. He watched me closely as I walked up the stairs. I have never seen anyone who could look at another so attentively. It was as if he let the whole being of the other man be built up before him in a subtle element of his own soul, while he himself remained immobile, in selfless surrender. It was not as if he were thinking about the other man, but there seemed to be a process of inner, spiritual reflecting in which his whole existence could be revealed."[17]

This complete "selfless surrender" can also be called love, and it carried in itself the germ for further development. The visitor felt an affirmation of his whole existence as he had never experienced it before. His very best sides, his highest aspirations had been perceived and strengthened. Steiner, having fathomed the full potential of the other, was subsequently sometimes disappointed in the actual performance of the man concerned, when the potential he had sensed was not realised and the other remained stuck in the limitations of his personality.

Everybody who came into close touch with him was amazed at Steiner's warmth and sensitivity. Richard Specht's testimony might be important because throughout his life he remained devoid of any interest in Anthroposophy and simply looked upon Steiner as an old friend. Richard was one of the four Specht boys whom Steiner had tutored in his Vienna days. (See *A Widened Environment*.) He became a well-known journalist and music critic, and was one of the earliest protagonists of Gustav Mahler. He wrote an obituary of Rudolf Steiner for one of the Vienna dailies, the *Journal*. In it he looked back on Steiner, the man and friend. "For my inner development I had no need of him and I went other ways." But he knew very well what the anthroposophical movement meant for Steiner and how much time and strength it demanded from him. Still, nothing "could stop him visiting my family every time he came to Vienna. His memory remained astonishingly correct. He remembered the smallest details of our common life and never wearied of enquiring after each one of us. But he never wanted to speak about, let alone discuss, anthroposophy."[18] It was clear that Specht was free to discuss spiritual matters if he so wished. But Steiner obviously enjoyed the undemanding social exchanges with Richard, he clearly did not wish to drop the relationship with a family who thirty years previously had so warmly embraced him. In his busy life he made time to cherish this connection. He met Richard and the rest of the family on the ground they themselves wished to choose. If they did not enquire into Steiner's innermost concerns, he was happy to discuss what matters were dear to them. No attempt at persuasion was made, freedom reigned and a friendship extended over a lifetime which other and lesser people might have dropped long before.

We can next look at the restrained description of the last encounter which Rittelmeyer had with Steiner.

"When I went to Dornach in May 1924 he came up to me after a lecture. He seemed like the spirit of kindness incarnate. When I want to realise what real kindness is I think of the picture of how he stood there before me, radiant with kindness and the light of the spirit. As we talked I saw, to my surprise, that he was obviously glad to speak of certain matters in the Anthroposophical Society which were sorely troubling him. He seemed almost overwhelmed by the shortcomings of his followers. But then he entered into my personal affairs just as if nothing else in the world mattered. As I was not feeling physically well he wanted me to speak in detail of what I had been going through. When I felt unwilling to do so even under pressure, because it seemed unimportant at that moment, he understood everything from the slightest indications.

"Only after his death did it dawn upon me that the last personal talk with him was actually a 'Farewell' in a deeper sense than was consciously realised at the time. He said a few words about me which seemed to express what he thought about our life's relation. They are too sacred for me to be able to tell them. I thanked him once again for having helped me from a distance with such effective advice in regard to my illness. He turned it off with an expression of infinite kindness:

'No, dear Herr Doctor, *I* thank *you* for having given me the opportunity to help.' Those were the last words he spoke to me on earth."[19]

Steiner knew equally well how to relate to a man of the spiritual calibre of Rittelmeyer and to ordinary folk. It gave him particular joy to lecture to the workmen of the Goetheanum – at their request, of course. He spoke to them in a most homely and direct way about matters of practical and esoteric significance and his diction was totally different from that of his evening lectures. He understood the mind of proletarians. When he addressed the work-forces of some factories on social questions, one of the eye-witnesses reported that tears were in their eyes and trust in their hearts.[20] Two episodes which Bely recounted show how in the most diverse situations Steiner responded fully and warm-heartedly. Mr and Mrs Bely had been invited to Steiner's house for supper. But suddenly Steiner disappeared. Twenty minutes later he returned with the first wild strawberries of the season which he had bought in a neighbouring village. – During the first World War a goodsized bunch of Swiss soldiers appeared in the Goetheanum area where building work was in full swing. More soldiers approached, cigarette in mouth. They wanted to see the building, but two anthroposophists explained to them that entry to the site was strictly prohibited. Bely realised that such behaviour would not do, invited the soldiers inside and ran to bring Steiner to the scene.

"We hurried together up the hill, already he stood among the soldiers, smiling, friendly, relaxed, and said that he would show them round. Together we entered the site. Cigarettes were extinguished. For half an hour he showed the soldiers around. At the end he climbed a scaffolding with them to show them the carved forms and demonstrate our way of working. 'I'd like to show you. Fetch a chisel and a hammer.' "[21] So he showed them and the soldiers were fascinated. "Their faces were open and joyful. Obviously they had difficulty in finding the right words to express their joy about the courteous humanity which Steiner had shown in this guided tour and his words of farewell."

Rittelmeyer's remark of the "selfless surrender" has already been quoted. He also described what such an attitude meant when translated into the minutiae of practical living. He went to Dornach for a short visit from Germany where inflation was raging.

"Dr Steiner had sent a car to the station and, as I had apparently missed the connection, a second one to meet the later train. He went with me to my lodging and saw to everything – whether the water supply was working, and whether there was a woman to clean the boots. In the evening after his lecture he came up and said to me: 'After all, I have forgotten to see about a charwoman for you. But I will do it now. She will be there early tomorrow morning.' Two days later when I was leaving again I was surprised to see him coming up the Dornach hill to meet me. He noticed that I was carrying our cases. 'Oh, I forgot to send someone to carry your luggage.' He looked around and beckoned to a young anthroposophist, waving my protest aside: 'He is very glad to do it.' Then he went with us into the canteen and sat down with us to breakfast, ordering the food himself from the serving table, and then once again when he realised that we needed provisions for the journey. After that he walked down the hill right to the station, chatting in the most friendly and interested way about various men, but also about protuberances on the sun. At the station he stood by the booking office window – I can still see that delicately built man standing there next to a corpulent monk – and stayed, still talking, until the train left. He was evidently anxious that as a poor German victim of inflation sickness I should have no expenses, but he did not make it in the least obvious. I said to myself at the time: This is really nothing to do with you as an individual. He would like to do the same to everyone. But that is impossible, and so he takes an opportunity like this to show what he would like to do for everyone."[22]

Selfless Surrender and Emphatic Expression

We have quoted more than once Rittelmeyer's words "Steiner's selfless surrender" to whomsoever he met and to the circumstances in which he found himself. But when he wished to state things publicly he was quite capable of a most impressive dynamism. This was already experienced in his pre-anthroposophic days. In Berlin Steiner had been on the committee of the Giordano Bruno Association which was interested in the social and practical consequences of a unitary view of the world. Another committee member, Hermann Friedmann, describes Steiner in his autobiography: "My great appreciation of his personality did not stem from any particular character trait, but from their relation to each other. My statement that he stood out in discussion should not be understood as if he talked a lot and talked impressively." He did this no more than others. "If he himself had not brought up the subject he said little or nothing. But he listened, he saw, felt and understood the speaker. This was admirable. But what was overwhelming for me was the relationship of this almost mystical silence – the completely open silence of the mystic in contrast to the silence of indifference – the relationship of this wordless listening to the dynamic power of his own speech on his own chosen subject." Only somebody who had observed Steiner's utter involvement when speaking and his selfless surrender when listening could truly appreciate him.[23]

Both these features are utterly important for the student of Steiner's works. He might still remember the strength with which Steiner rejects Plato's dualism when he comes upon a passage in which Steiner speaks of the same man with the deepest respect. Equally he might be puzzled when Steiner speaks with strength and personal commitment about a particular attitude and later finds equally strong and convincing words about an apparently opposite attitude. Lukewarm he could never be. He was too involved in each particular situation. Not that he personally wanted or expected anything. But by giving his concentration to any particular attitude he could also appreciate it to the full, he surrendered to it. Turgeneva describes Steiner directing a rehearsal of a Christmas play. He shows how he wants Joseph to be played. Suddenly an old man he stumbles over the stage with vacant expression. He slips and falls. The actors frightened run to help him, but he jumps up and laughs. "That's how Joseph should be played." And Turgeneva adds: "It was incredible – this ability to change."[24]

But this attitude of selfless surrender goes much further. Lehrs describes Steiner's behaviour during a chemistry lesson in the *Waldorfschule*.[25] Steiner is as curious as the children who watch the ongoing experiment, as attentive as they and as frightened when the oxyhydrogen gas explodes with a loud bang. When Steiner in his autobiography describes this attitude of selfless surrender he modestly calls it "being another person's guest." In Weimar the other people were, not surprisingly, unable to understand his own position. But he was able to emphasise and identify with them, he was 'on a visit' within the totality of their existence.

Practically everybody who was able to have a private conversation with Steiner felt this selfless surrender with astonishment and amazement. The man opposite seemed to understand everything, he spoke to him as nobody had spoken to him before. The visitor felt ennobled. He had indeed found a lover of men.

The Breath of Freedom

In his pre-anthroposophical days Steiner had laid particular stress on the freedom of the individual. As long as man obeys even the highest precepts he is not truly free. Now he was regarded by many as a spiritual teacher whose every word had to be taken in, and if possible, utilised, followed, obeyed. It was a situation which could easily have become disastrous. The fact is that Steiner suffered terribly from among other things, a blind belief in him on the part of some of his followers. In Rittelmeyer's words:

"Such is the tragedy that is bound up with greatness, a tragedy that will always be there when a great man appears. But Rudolf Steiner never failed to let it be known that the men he liked best were those who stood before him in freedom and self-assurance. Even wilfulness did not altogether displease him, although he could not regard it as a quality likely to promote the cause of Anthroposophy. The way in which he combined the pressing need of the cause with respect for personal freedom always called forth my unqualified admiration. If it were a matter of choosing he always put the freedom of a man before the needs of the cause. For he regarded the future temple of mankind as lost if it were built upon medieval foundations."[26]

Bely made the same point: "Many people could not grasp until Steiner's death that 'the teacher' should not have interfered in the decisions of his pupils. And what about those anthroposophists who are chained hand and foot to Steiner's statements? To them I can only offer my deepest conviction that anybody who fettered himself to Steiner can never have been his pupil. Such people were members of the Anthroposophical Society from which the Teacher of Freedom could never have barred them, but he did not have to be a member of it."[27] We shall see later how Steiner faced this dilemma in the Society which he eventually founded himself. (See Chapter Nine.)

Bely went on to give a concrete example, his first meeting with Steiner. He had gone to ask Steiner whether he should enter on the traditional path of esoteric discipline. He wanted his advice "because I was convinced of his honesty and integrity". Bely realised that his question was double-edged. Steiner must have noticed the immense confidence which this brilliant young writer placed in him. If Steiner encouraged him it would mean interfering in the other man's decision who, on the whole, was quite attracted to the traditional path. Steiner chose not to answer.

"I shall never forget my shock: A man travels from Brussels to
Cologne to ask for advice. This man takes half an hour to put before
Steiner the earnest and grave reasons which made him come and ask
whether or not he could entrust himself to those to whom he feels
attracted and who appear to him his true teachers. – Steiner's role is
felt not that of a teacher, but of an honest counsellor – and the answer
is deadly silence."

But for Steiner this silence meant following the rule which he had
laid down for himself and which he had suggested also for those who
want to take his advice in esoteric matters: "Formulate each of your
words so that you do not interfere in the free decision of another
person." Bely's narrative continues:

"After a long interval: 'Are you perhaps free in July?', – 'Yes.' –
'Would you perhaps like to come to Munich? Come and see us. In
Munich we might have more time to go into these questions." A very
worldly, open invitation of one independent person to another equally
independent. But it was no answer to my direct question in which
there might have been a sly temptation as in the question of the
Pharisees to Christ whether it was right to pay tribute to Caesar."[28]

Stresses and Strains

These two testimonies, by two people as different from each other as
Rittelmeyer and Bely, are of greatest importance both for an
appreciation of the man Rudolf Steiner and for a true understanding
of his work and of the Society which he founded. Such an attitude
would be highly respected in anyone leading the life of a
contemplative. But Steiner lived *in* the world, exposed himself to all
its suffering and actively attempted to shape and form it. It certainly
needed special social skills to deal with the sort of situation which
occasionally impinged upon Steiner's own sphere of discretion. One
or more anthroposophists might have done something socially naive
or even outrageous, perhaps pretending at the same time that they had
done it in the name of Steiner and for the good of his movement. In
such cases, particularly if others had been hurt in the process, he
could be unusually forthright and uncompromising in his public
condemnation. To the amazement of many Steiner could five minutes
later talk in the most charming and affirmative manner to the person
he had apparently condemned. But he had not condemned any
person, he had condemned an action or an attitude. He supported the

person, knowing full well man's fallible nature. This unusual, but exemplary form of behaviour was for many anthroposophists a model. It also must have strained Steiner's inner discipline to the utmost. Bely describes a devastating meeting in Dornach where Steiner with the full force of his personality had to censure certain social malpractices. Bely and his wife had a long-standing invitation to supper with Steiner immediately after this disastrous meeting.

"We felt our invitation was an anachronism. It seemed our visit was like bursting into a house where a dead man had been laid out. The dead man was the Anthroposophical Society which Steiner had brought into existence. We felt oppressed and let him and Marija Jacovlevna (Marie Steiner) go ahead after the meeting, following slowly and rang the bell. Still oppressed, we entered as if a house of mourning. But from the landing we saw Steiner sitting in the brightly coloured dining room. Around the table stood large, very decorative red chairs. Steiner still in his coat sat in one of these chairs and took off his boots, – it had been muddy outside. He looked up to Miss Waller who probably had said something funny, and he laughed happily like a child. On the table there was a bunch of roses and I remember how, as he saw us standing on the landing he waved to us from behind the roses to join him in the dining room . . . The whole evening Steiner was in a happy, jocular mood. There was much laughter and joking as if to encourage us."[29]

Again we find this "selfless surrender" to people and to social situations. We can marvel at the absoluteness with which Steiner gave himself to every moment of his life and equally we may marvel at the strain such total involvement must have caused him, a strain completely absent from the life of the Christian contemplative or the Eastern guru. Bely compared him to Paul, who said of himself that he had been all things to all men. "When I hear Paul's cry he had been all things to all men in order to wake up but a few, I can say to myself: indeed, I can understand you. For I have seen Steiner."[30] This is, however, only the one pole of Steiner's way of meeting people. The other is the overwhelming peace which he radiated and which he bestowed on each intimate meeting.

The Spiritual Dimension

It is to the spiritual dimension in Steiner that we now turn. Here it will be necessary to make fuller use of quotations than so far. His spiritual potency made, of course, the most profound impression on those around him, but it needed a spiritually inclined and extremely literate partner adequately to articulate this impression. A teacher from the *Waldorfschule* who saw Steiner fairly frequently states that his most shattering experience of Steiner was the way in which the latter rose from his seat and listened in deepest reverence as a lesson from the Gospels was read to the children during a Sunday service.[31]

Only few people were able to witness such examples of Steiner's profound religiosity. He, in truth, went 'to his closet' and scrupulously avoided making a show of his devotion. It is generally understood that every afternoon at three o'clock he spoke the Latin Lord's Prayer in a loud voice. Lehrs reports[32] how on one of his nocturnal car journeys Steiner was handed a cup of coffee. He did not drink it all, but "with slight movement of hand and arm he poured the rest on the earth, a marvellous gesture of libation, of letting the earth participate in the enlivening substance." Lehrs then goes on to tell us how on railway journeys Steiner always broke the first sandwich handed to him and shared it with his neighbour.

Other descriptions go much further and cannot be summarised. Rittelmeyer remembered what he felt during the first intimate lecture which he attended. Again and again he asked himself "Whoever are you?"

"Every test the human mind could make, provided it was an unprejudiced one, came out in favour of the miraculous. Healthy-mindedness? It would have no more convincing form than this. Any suggestion of mental abnormality – and as a clergyman I had a great many cases of this kind to deal with – would have been given the lie by the very atmosphere. Moral purity? We were living and breathing in it. Selflessness? – If one asked oneself: What must a freely bestowed gift of the gods be like? – It could not be different from this. But then, what was it all? The beginning of human majesty as yet undreamed of? A message from a higher world sent at the right hour? Those born in after centuries will hardly be able to realise the feelings of those of us who had been living in materialism and witnessed events like this. Already today we see before us a growing generation who seem to find no difficulty in what seemed to us to be mighty hammer blows against the world edifice in which we were living."[33]

Rittelmeyer was a very careful observer and he knew Steiner over more than one decade. So he was in a position to indicate Steiner's spiritual progress over this time:

"In earlier years it seemed to me that when he was giving advice to people he liked to sit where he would not be obliged to look against the light. When he began to use his faculties of spiritual sight one noticed a certain deliberate adjustment of his being, often accompanied by a lowering of the eyes. One remembered then what he says in his books, namely, that the physical body of a man must be wiped out before the higher members can be perceived. As the years went on I noticed this less and less, and finally not at all. He seemed to pass without effort into the higher state of consciousness; or rather it was as if both states of consciousness, that of sense perception and of spiritual perception, were there for him freely and naturally, one beside the other. In the same way, on several occasions in earlier years I thought I often noticed that at the beginning of a conversation it was not easy for him to find the right words. One said to oneself then that he had surely been occupied with his spiritual investigations and needed a few seconds for the transition to the world of purely physical existence. He tried to find the appropriate word, missed it and stopped. A brief effort – and the difficulty was overcome. This, too, I noticed less and less frequently as time went on. In the early years there were sometimes moments in a lecture when one would have the impression – now he is occupied with some intervening spiritual observation. At such moments he would speak hesitatingly, letting the sentence slowly finish itself, and sometimes even padding it. Later on, one often saw from his very look – which could change with rapidity as the result of mighty spiritual impulses – that extraordinary things were going on within him, far more extraordinary than were actually said. And yet the two aspects did not seem separate but rather to be livingly united. When I thought about the development which Rudolf Steiner himself manifested – in so far as I was able to perceive it – it seemed to me amazingly rapid, and to put the others of us to shame. – It is not fair to the world to withhold these observations. But I myself would not like them to be regarded as authoritative unless they are compared with those made by others as well."[34]

Rittelmeyer's book is of the greatest value for those who want to realise what Steiner was like as a man of body, soul and spirit. The same is true of Bely's work. Both were highly intelligent and critical observers, both were spiritually sensitive and also socially very much aware. Bely was the greater writer and, possibly, even more sensitive than Rittelmeyer. Bely lived for a few years in close physical proximity to Steiner. Rittelmeyer was treated by Steiner almost like a junior colleague to whom he could openly speak about some of his own concerns, assured that the other would understand. Once Steiner told him about the death of an anthroposophist. He had visited him, but "when I arrived death had already crept up to the throat. I fought with death all through the night and have been defeated." Rittelmeyer was amazed about such tenacity. Steiner's simple reply was "Can one do otherwise?"[35]

Rittelmeyer then tells of another occasion when Steiner had wanted to meet him to discuss arrangements for the funeral of another man. Steiner said: "This morning before I was up" the man in question "came and said farewell. Twenty minutes afterwards a messenger came with the news of his death." Rittelmeyer though at first perplexed had the sense to ask what it feels like when a dead man says farewell. Steiner said with a smile: "Oh, it is just as when a man comes into the room on some other occasion. He simply comes and says farewell. During the first hours after death it is quite easy to see such a thing. After that it becomes more difficult."[36]

A third instance of Steiner's awareness of the dead indicates also his caution in a case which he had not checked and checked again, and also his sensitive concern for third parties. Rittelmeyer wanted to know whether Steiner had ever met his – Rittelmeyer's – dead mother. "When you are listening to a lecture", is Steiner's reply, "an individuality often comes whom *I take to be* your mother. She brings others with her. She is a little restless and moves to and fro. But she takes the deepest interest in your spiritual life." Then turning to Mrs Rittelmeyer he all but apologises for not having been able to contact her dead father.[37]

The next two examples are to illustrate two different things: the objective, scientific way in which Steiner speaks about occult facts and some of Rittelmeyer's experiences on the esoteric path which we shall discuss more fully later. (See Chapter Six.) Nevertheless, it seems better to treat both aspects in conjunction and refer back to them at the appropriate time than to divide these two incidents into statements of fact on the one hand and Rittelmeyer's comments on them on the other.

"I once dreamt that I asked Dr Steiner: 'Who were you in your previous incarnation?' He answered: 'Pythagoras and Menander.' – When I woke up the experience remained vividly with me. I asked myself whether there could be any truth in it. Pythagoras – yes, that might be a possibility, although up to that moment the idea had never consciously occurred to me. But Menander – who was he? I looked in the encyclopaedia and found two Menanders, one a poet and writer of comedies and the other a rhetorician. But they both lived so close to the time of Pythagoras that it was not easy to reconcile the suggestion with other anthroposophical views on the subject. Was it perhaps King Milinda who had the remarkable discourse with Buddha? – A few weeks later I was able to speak to Dr Steiner and I told him about the dream experience. He first asked when it had happened and I told him almost exactly. 'It has nothing to do with my incarnations,' he said. 'But that night I was deeply occupied with the study of Pythagoras and Menander, not only in a scientific sense.' 'Which Menander was it?' I asked, curious as to whether Dr Steiner knew of the two of whose existence I had only learned from the encyclopaedia. 'It was the rhetorician. I was working at a problem concerned with speech and tried to get into contact with him.' Incidents like this give food for thought in many directions. To me the main significance was that I saw clearly how easily errors creep into spiritual experiences of this kind. For on the face of it the actual spiritual impression was: Steiner, Pythagoras, Menander. But immediately the question about earlier incarnations cropped up. This came from a half-unconscious curiosity complex within me. And yet it was through this complex that the experience became strong enough to be reflected by the consciousness. When I was thinking about the experience afterwards I could clearly distinguish the different spiritual character of the two regions – that of interest mixed with curiosity and that of objective fact. And so I had the first basic standards for discriminating between true and false spiritual experiences. It was borne in upon me how right Dr Steiner was when he indicated that nobody can receive reliable impressions of the world of spirit who has not passed the 'Guardian of the Threshold' and has not learned so completely to scrutinise his whole inner life that he can recognise the elements shooting in from the personal side of his being."[38]

There is no need for further comment. The following passage however, can do with a short introduction. Steiner's description of the totality of the human being includes an 'etheric body', a field of formative, shaping forces, forces of which we can become aware in ourselves if we undertake certain exercises or are unusually gifted naturally, and which can also be observed in others. Rittelmeyer had taken up such exercises and had realised that such an 'etheric body' really exists.

"It has its own centres which do not exactly coincide with the physical organs, and are distinguished from these by a much more spiritual sense of life. This body also has its own currents of life which to a certain extent a man can learn to control. He can become aware of his own life body and then clearly perceive where it is more highly and where it is less developed. I was burning to know if Dr Steiner saw in a man the same things he can know out of himself. According to his writings it must certainly be so. But perhaps he said what was true *not* as the outcome of direct perception but because he could in some ways read what the human being in front of him was thinking and expecting, getting it from the consciousness of the other. And so I tried to safeguard myself against this. At home I fixed firmly in my mind my own impressions of what was still undeveloped and what showed signs of developing, and then I deliberately killed all these thoughts. As if by chance I then asked Dr Steiner about the life body and tried desperately to think about other matters. But it was almost frightening how he began to describe with the precision and assurance of a scientific investigator who has an object before him, things which I alone could have known. In spite of this my caution was not yet satisfied. A year later I repeated the experiment. The incentive was the greater because in the intervening period a great deal had changed in this life body, was indeed quite reversed. Again I fortified myself and began to ask questions. On this and all other occasions Dr Steiner went into them willingly and without hesitation. Perhaps he would say now and then: 'I know of course that you are asking this out of a sincere interest in knowing the truth.' On this particular occasion when I had put my questions he began at once with the words: 'To my surprise a great deal has changed. I had not expected this.'...And again he described with the precision of the scientist, only making what I already knew still clearer to me. I know, of course, that a scientist of today cannot yet regard experiences of this kind as 'proof'. On the other hand I know that a young generation to whom spiritual truths come much more naturally will not quite understand why one felt it necessary to make such tests. Yet I am glad that I did not neglect them. And I have every reason for thinking that Rudolf Steiner was not annoyed by my attitude but, on the contrary, that he was glad to be met with cautious personal investigation. Experiences like this – which were repeated many times – gradually melted the feeling of mistrust which at the beginning one seemed bound to maintain. And although the same attitude of alertness and critical investigation was maintained on every subsequent occasion there was quite sufficient inducement and indeed a sense of obligation to continue one's investigations along these paths."[39]

Where spiritual powers abound and a strong personal relationship exists, help is possible even beyond the limits which normally apply. Bely – whose real name was Bugayev – gives us two striking accounts of help received. They also illustrate one of Steiner's greatest dilemmas: how to give help without causing dependence.

"In Munich in the autumn of 1913 I had to face strong inner struggles. But he appeared decidedly indifferent, even stern. In his glance there was reproach. Later I realised he knew what I was doing. He wanted me out of my own resources to discover the roots of the evil within us. One day, during a concert the image of myself arose in me. Filled with bitterness I was ready to surrender. Suddenly in the first row Steiner rose and looked at me so that this moment of self-knowledge became a source of light."[40]

"In the spring of 1915, I think it was March, somebody tapped me fairly strongly on the shoulder as I was leaving the studio after a lecture. I turned around and there was Steiner close behind me. Very serious, very kind, almost like a father he winked at me and said: 'Courage, Mr Bugayev, no fear.' But what was I to fear? I had doubts, I suffered, I was bewildered, but I had no fear. The reason appeared later. My state of anxiety lasted for months. In this dark time my constant attitude was turned towards him imploring him for help. But he did not seem to hear me. Repeatedly, between April and August indescribable attacks of anxiety befell me. Steiner had foreseen them and when he had approached me and tapped me on the shoulder he had armed me for the incipient battle against the spectre of anxiety."[41]

Faith

The reality of such events is further underlined by the following narration of Anna Samweber. She was a very down-to-earth woman who for some years lived in Steiner's house in Berlin. Her life was full of dramatic events, some of them in connection with Steiner. She displayed the attitude of Faith in the sense in which the earliest Christians understood it: an unshakable conviction of the *constant* presence and *overwhelming* effect of the spiritual powers within and around us. The place of this particular event was Berlin, the time a cold, foggy evening in November. A certain errand brought Miss Samweber to a lonely building site.

"Suddenly, out of the dark appeared two figures and fell upon me. Rudolf Steiner had once said that in an emergency I could always turn to him. As the two ruffians dashed at me and the one held me from behind so that the other could rob me I called spontaneously, but silently: 'Help me, Doctor.' At this moment the two gave a jerk as if stung by some poisonous insect and were gone. When next morning Rudolf Steiner came for breakfast and saw me he said: 'Good morning, Sam. You *did* shout loudly last night. What happened?' I told him. He listened quietly and said very simply and comfortingly: 'So I have been able to help you after all.' "[42]

Earlier on, we spoke of the unlimited extent of Steiner's compassion and three paragraphs above of the ensuing dilemma: how to give help without causing dependence. (See *A Lover of Men*.) Another fact increased this dilemma. If one is able to foresee the future in its actuality or in its potentiality to what extent is one allowed to interfere without misusing one's gifts and putting other people in a state of unfreedom and dependence? Steiner repeatedly mentioned this dilemma and stated that you can either know the future or try to shape it: he had chosen the latter course. "It would not do to investigate these things by occult means and then allow the knowledge so gained to colour one's actions."[43] But the actual problems which his life presented him with were so complicated and varied that this basic formula had to be subtly differentiated. Usually he gave his advice very gently so that people never felt compelled to follow it. Cases were frequent where people said 'If only I had followed his advice . . .' 'If only I knew then what I know now . . .' which testify to his restraint as much as to his insight. Yet the present writer knows of two occasions where, at the express wish of the two men concerned, Steiner gave explicit practical instructions of what they were to do in critical situations. When, however, he himself was involved he was unable to take preventive action. On more than one occasion he had hinted that the first Goetheanum would not stand for long. – It is even possible that the first realisation of possible disaster came on the day before he decided to build. – Early in December 1922 Steiner paid a short visit to Berlin. Miss Samweber, who had never seen the building had an intense wish to go to Dornach for the Christmas conference, but was unable to do so without Steiner's help. He was unable to meet her wish and promised help for the Easter conference. But she burst out: "If I cannot go now I shall never see the building. We are going to lose it. It will burn to the ground and will no longer exist at Easter." Steiner must have been impressed by the strength of conviction with which his old and trusted friend spoke. It was another case of 'Faith'. But he only "looked at me with wide eyes, did not for a moment refer to this statement of mine and again promised help for Easter. At the moment he was unable to help, he said, and I would have to look out for another possibility."[44] An opportunity arose and Samweber took it eagerly. Towards the end of December she arrived in Dornach. During a walk in the afternoon she told her two companions of her premonitions. "After this statement Herr Gern thought I was not normal."[45] The same night the building was burnt down.

It appears that after the warning was received Steiner did not take any special precautions. He had to live under the same conditions as all other human beings. His responsibilities were infinitely larger, his concerns infinitely wider, but his predicament no less grave than that of his fellow men. He fully accepted the human condition and avoided meticulously not only creating unfreedom and dependence, but also anything that came near to spiritual manipulation, to magic. The present writer knows, however, of one occasion when Steiner used his unusual faculties, innocently enough, for his own advantage. W. J. Stein who told this story was at the time of the event in his late twenties. He was close to Steiner and on the occasion in question accompanied him on a car journey. It was a winter's evening and they were passing through a town. Steiner suddenly stopped the car, went into a bookshop and soon returned with a book which he showed with great joy to Stein. He had needed this book for a long time, he explained. Stein asked how he knew that this rare book was obtainable here. "I happened to see it in the shop window", was the reply. However, this was a physical impossibility. The car was in motion, the light was poor. His 'seeing' had obviously not been our seeing.

Everyday Affairs

It is remarkable that a man of such spiritual power had learned to live so completely *in* the world as it presents itself to the consciousness of contemporary men. He was unusually well informed about political and cultural events. Rittelmeyer reports a number of incidents to show how closely Steiner observed the flow of events during the first

World War[46] and how correct his judgment was. "In all the things Dr Steiner said to me during the War, this" – the Pope's peace initiative – was the only "point where he proved to be not entirely correct."

He loved to have his meals in company and in a relaxed, social atmosphere. Serious subjects were rarely discussed during mealtimes. Samweber – the only person who gave a few details of what living in the same house as Steiner was like – mentions occasions when the pressures on Steiner showed. "I too must have my occasional grumble and I must grumble about people of whom I know they can take it."[47] And at another occasion: "I too am a human being after all." He loved humour, particularly during meals, and liked to play the occasional practical joke. W. J. Stein, a highly intelligent man, courageous and self-confident, but not particularly gifted in the artistic field, told this story: He happened to be in Dornach and asked Steiner about the meaning of the glass windows of the Goetheanum. He could appreciate the rest of the building, he felt, but the windows baffled him. In reply Steiner invited him to join a group of people whom he would show round the building in the afternoon. Stein duly came and joined the group. When they reached the windows Steiner said: "Ladies and gentlemen, I would like to introduce you to my friend, Dr Stein. He will now explain to you what these windows are meant to illustrate." Stein probably rose to the occasion.

We end where we began: To whom can we compare Rudolf Steiner? What do we call him? A scientist of the spirit? A lover of his fellow men? A seer? An initiate? A spiritual revolutionary? Surely, none of these terms does justice to the full reality. 'An outstanding man' is too vague. Perhaps: a man who showed in the twentieth century the full potential of what it means to be human. It might be best to leave the summing up to somebody else, M. Jules Sauerwein. He, a contemporary of Steiner's, was an outstanding French journalist on the staff of *Le Matin* and had unusually close relations to a number of French governments. When once asked who was the most interesting man whom he had met in his career he replied: "I have known almost all monarchs on earth, almost all prime ministers and military leaders. But nobody was able to make such a lasting impression on me as the Austrian philosopher and occultist Rudolf Steiner. He was the most interesting man I ever met . . . However powerful the statesmen were they always struck me as actors not quite sure of their parts. But what delight to talk politics with Steiner. Only so great and all-embracing an intellect is able to penetrate individual problems so correctly."[48]

The Lecturer: An Appendix

A study of the man Steiner would be incomplete without looking at him as a lecturer. During his lectures sensitive people were able to experience directly how the various strands of his being combined to build up a constantly changing and powerful spiritual event. Today, the transcripts of his more than 6000 lectures are available in print. But it would be a grievous mistake were we to look upon these transcripts as lectures in the usual meaning of the term. Certainly, this was not the impression of the people who witnessed the reality of the lectures. They often felt they were present at a form of divine service, an act in which the boundaries between earth and heaven had temporarily vanished. Steiner, as we have seen, also felt that his lectures were not suitable material for print. (See end *Increasing Activity*.) He looked on them as seeds which like the Sower in the Gospels he scattered freely. The fruits would depend on the human soil in which they fell. Many would wither, but others bear fruit a thousandfold. There would not be a uniform harvest, but each sprout would be itself, a huge variety of blooms and blossoms, but fortified, encouraged and stimulated by the action of the sower. Steiner, of course, never referred to the Gospels when speaking about himself. Typically, he turned to science. Nature is prolific and wasteful. Only one herring's egg out of a hundred will be fertilised, all the others are wasted. He too will only fertilise the few, but in order to do so must speak to many.

His instrument was the living 'Word' manifest not only in articulated concepts, but also in intonation and sound, gesture and glance, which together would fuse into a unique mood generated by the speaker. People have confirmed that in this situation the conceptual part of Steiner's message was clear and convincing while this might not be so when later they re-read the same message in cold print. This was not due simply to the effect of an unusual personality, but mainly to an 'objective' factor, Steiner's faculty of complete surrender. He *became* what he expressed. Bely was sensitive enough to realise this even before Steiner had begun to speak.

"Sometimes the content of the lecture was already shining through Steiner's mood: the tenor of the lecture which was as yet unknown to us. I had the impression I was able to sense in advance the basic tenor of the lectures like an aura that floated around his face. Often I thought when I saw him standing there in the attitude described:

Important words about Christ will be spoken. Something preceded the event, something descended upon him. He seemed stern, but also full of warmth, I would dare to say, even hot. The colour of his face, the invisible one, visible only to a refined form of consciousness, was warm almost like the hot scarlet of glowing roses. Of course, what I am saying now is subjective. Not subjective is for me the fact that in certain periods of my life when I was close to Steiner I correctly guessed the key of the still unknown lecture. I perceived the glowing scarlet and the stern, benevolent and devout love which radiated from his forehead, his larynx and his chest, I perceived those, independent of the colour of his face, as expressing: We are going to speak of Christ.

"As soon as he stood behind the lectern the basic note of the lecture became ever clearer to me. It was accompanied by a subjective colour perception, an aura as it were. A definite atmosphere spread around him in all directions. Its colour and tone were clearly perceptible to me. Of course, I am not speaking of the optical, but an inward perception. But with greatest reliability it was always sent to me like a telegram before the beginning of the lecture. It was as if he always had a particular aura. Apart from the glowing red of his words about Christ this aura could be of a rose-coloured gold, of brilliant white, or pink and white."[49]

Bely continues to say that similar changes could be perceived in his face, its colour and inner gesture. In the end Steiner was enveloped by a definite entity. In Bely's words he had built himself a 'hut', an invisible, but manifest tabernacle in which the act now to begin could be celebrated. It was an act demanding a conscious effort of a kind which seems to go to the limits of human possibilities. He attempted to weave together into an articulated and distinctly shaped whole three strands of multiple relationships which impinged on him more or less simultaneously: the relationship to spiritual facts and beings, the source of what he had to say, the relationship to various people in his audience, the pole to which the whole dynamic effort was to flow, and the relationship to the earthly conditions beyond the lecture room, the unique situation of the place and time of an individual lecture. We shall now look in turn at each of these relationships.

Immediacy

Occasionally, Steiner gave us indications of the nature of his lectures. One such passage occurs in a Dornach lecture.[50] He explains there that he cannot prepare his material before the lecture or speak from memory, but only from the immediate experience, his sensing or 'seeing'. Therefore it is just as difficult for him to speak about a certain subject for the thirtieth as for the first time. His "preparation is a kind of spiritual exercise" (*Üben*) . . . A precondition for his producing the lecture was quiet, peace and concentration. These were commodities in short supply and he gently complained about the insensitivity of some anthroposophists who ask all sorts of questions before a lecture without realising "that in the next moment facts have to be garnered from the spiritual world." His concentrated preparation consisted of creating a mood which was to enable him to be in touch with one particular aspect of the spiritual world while all other aspects remained unperceived. He speaks about this remarkable 'filtering effect' which enables him to focus on the same spiritual texture from ever new sides.[51]

What he discovers there are, of course, no *physical* facts or actions. Everything is personalised, so what he perceives are thoughts, intentions, motivations of beings.[52] Nothing is static. "A truth grasped in the spirit cannot be delineated in sharp contours because it is something mobile"[53] and alive. But to give spiritual experiences clear outlines is exactly what Steiner was attempting to do in his lectures. They are not personal reactions of a visionary, but the conscious efforts of a spiritual researcher to present his findings in an objective form. In this attempt he was handicapped by the limitations of education and of language. In his endeavour to convey spiritual experiences in conceptual guise he can only use those concepts which he himself had learned in school or had come across later. Sometimes they might be more of a hindrance than a help.[54] Even the very words he is bound to use will distort what he wishes to say. They are meant to describe physical, three-dimensional existence and therefore "are powerless to express the many-layered nature of the impulses of reality."[55] Words fetter us. Their meanings and their emotional content were often defined by bygone ages. Ideally, he would have loved to create his words always anew.

Again we come across the unique nature of Steiner. All through history and in all known cultures people have existed who had intimations of the spirit. They either reacted emotionally to them, personally, often with their consciousness greatly dimmed down, or they recollected in tranquillity experiences they had long ago. Steiner hoped that other people would freely use his experiences. So they had to have an objective character, they had to be reshaped with the help of the inadequate medium of human concepts and human words. Often he despaired, the task seemed all but impossible of achievement. Occasionally he was so overwhelmed by the grandeur and power of his experience that he faltered and apologised for his stumbling words. Some such moments are recounted by Bely.[56] There Bely speaks of a man, one among the greatest, completely overwhelmed by the majesty of the spirit, of the world of God, of the love of Christ.

Relation to Audience

We have already seen that Steiner was able to perceive Rittelmeyer's dead mother approaching her son as he listened to Steiner's words. (See *The Spiritual Dimension.*) This contact to members of his audience was nothing unique to this occasion. We can safely assume that it was the rule, not the exception. When reading Steiner's lectures we often notice that the content of the first page or two is fairly thin. It is the time when he *senses* his audience. We have many examples of how he addressed a lecture to *one* person, particularly to a newcomer to his lectures. An illuminating and detailed example is known from Prague. A woman went for the first time to hear Steiner who was giving a public lecture. She seated herself in about the eighth row. About ten minutes after the beginning of the lecture she noticed Steiner's eye resting on her for a moment. Gradually the subject of the lecture changed and when the woman left the room she had 'recognised' Steiner. For he had given her the answer to the main problem which occupied her mind at this time and on which her thoughts had centred as she entered the lecture room.

Heinz Müller was a young man in the first War where he was seriously wounded. During a series of operations he had some unusual experiences which he could not understand. He was advised to see Steiner and had a number of most intimate conversations with him. One of his questions was deferred. Steiner wanted to give this answer at a later date. During a lecture Müller's question was answered in detail and he went afterwards to thank Steiner for his answer. "I am so glad you heard it",[57] was the reply. Later Müller found that his friends had no recollection of this passage, and when after some years, the lecture appeared in print no reference was to be found to the answer which Müller had received.

In a lecture during the War Steiner once made some remarks about this intimate relationship to his audience. Some time ago he had spoken about the positive aspects of the German people and this had been a great comfort to his audience who knew how other Europeans looked at them during that time. Some people subsequently came to Steiner and asked him whether he would not say the same when next he addressed Frenchmen. He replied that this was impossible. He had to speak "as things come alive within me while I am standing in front of just *you*. For I speak this not out of *my*, but out of *your* hearts as well as I am just able to do it." He serves the spirit by excluding himself and articulating what lives in the souls of his listeners.[58]

This second relationship, the relationship to his audience, needs some comment. Obviously Steiner did not give lectures to reveal the contents of the subconscious of one or more of his listeners. But he was intensely aware of the expectations, prejudices and emotions of his audience. They made him not only change the subject of a particular lecture, but they also helped to determine its mood and its detailed conduct. Steiner spoke *out of,* and not *in opposition to* the prevailing mood of his audience unless, of course, circumstances made a confrontation imperative. But then also the first relationship, that to the spiritual world, was absent.

A conversation which Rittelmeyer had re-inforces the point. It was during the War and Rittelmeyer's congregation in the Protestant Church were unhappy about his apparent lack of nationalism, his inability to hate. Steiner told him it was no use telling the congregation: Don't hate, love the English. "This will only upset them and won't help." Rather he should say: "When the German fights, he never hates the person, he hates the *cause.*"[59] This shows that Steiner took the emotional state of his various audiences as a thing given. He would work with it and attempt to raise this state to a higher level, to sublimate it.

This helps us to appreciate the great diversity of the emotional content and mood of Steiner's lectures as well as some passages in the lectures which strike the present-day reader as not entirely happy. "Some things had to remain unsaid because of the loose life of Mr X during the last days, some had to be repeated for the sake of the old lady who had specially come to this lecture from a neighbouring town."[60]

These two activities, the articulation of encounters with spiritual entities which took place there and then in front of the audience, and the other, the constant sensing and keeping in mind of the psychological and spiritual condition of his listeners went on at the same time. "We knew that in those moments when the radiant aspect of Steiner's dialogue with the higher world stood out, his perceptivity of the manifestations of the physical plane of reality was not dimmed, but sharpened. It was just in these moments that he recognised the most hidden depths of each of us."[61]

The third relationship, that to the space and time in which a lecture was given, forms usually more of a background. It tinges the mood of a lecture, and is rarely absent. Occasionally, though, it breaks through with overpowering force. An outstanding example is the Vienna lecture of 14th April, 1914. This is the last lecture of a course in which Steiner spoke perhaps more gently and intimately about man's life after his physical death than at any other occasion. But suddenly, towards the end of this last lecture he speaks in an unusually harsh and cutting way about the awful, death-bringing cancer which besets present-day mankind: our economic life at the mercy of market forces. A careful reading of the lecture as well as some references made by Steiner in later years make it clear that here was a prophetic vision of the War which was to break out only a few months later and through events at the place where Steiner was then speaking. Is it reasonable to assume that at this moment the 'filtering effect' broke down and a completely unexpected and horrifying perspective opened up before his spiritual eye?

PART II
The Teaching

Chapter Three
A Philosopher of Freedom

Before entering into a discussion of Steiner as a teacher of the Spirit it might seem right to take stock of his views as published before 1900. They are contained mainly in four books, *Goethe's World View, A Theory of Knowledge, Truth and Knowledge,* and *The Philosophy of Freedom,*[1] and in the articles written for the *Magazin.* Together they deal with social renewal, the autonomous moral personality, and a theory of knowledge which takes as its starting point Goethe's scientific writings. He arrives at the view that the true act of knowing is tantamount to a communion in which the world and man are reunited.

Already at the age of about twenty Steiner had written: "I feel called upon to spread light on one part of Goethe's spiritual achievement."[2] This occupation with Goethe had important consequences for Steiner. He had always had the gift of experiencing, 'seeing' the physical-spiritual totality of the world, – so much so that he only very gradually learned to deal with the world of lifeless objects.[3] Goethe showed him a different way: how a meticulous, patient observation of the *physical* aspect of reality leads gradually to an awareness of its spiritual dimension. Such observation needs utter concentration and imagination, a freeing of sensual reality from its usual conceptual mould. This combination of concentration and imagination is, however, very close to meditation as Steiner later came to teach it. Steiner, on the other hand, had already at school discovered the spiritual importance of thinking, not only in establishing truth, but also as a mental and spiritual *activity*. This enabled him to draw philosophical conclusions from the experience which he shared with Goethe, the spiritual unity of man and the universe. This is an experience almost universally described by oriental thinkers. Modern people in search of truth are often unaware of the great part this experience has also played in European cultural history.

When Steiner rationally looked at this unity of man and universe he began to question the conviction of modern Europeans that our thoughts in some mysterious way are 'subjective'. In fact, they are quite naturally the product of one integral part of the universe. He himself was convinced that they belong to reality as much as the realm of the senses. In the fusion of 'pure perception' and 'pure concept' man restores the original unity of the universe. In other words, he achieves an act of communion between himself and the creative forces of the world. These and related thoughts represent the philosophical basis of Anthroposophy[4], but they have rarely penetrated beyond its confines. The reason may be that Steiner wrote his theory of knowledge just before such theories became unfashionable and philosophers turned instead to the discussion of scientific methodology. Steiner used the vocabulary of German idealistic philosophy which under the influence of logical positivism and linguistic analysis lost ground everywhere, not least in Central Europe. These historical facts may explain the neglect of Steiner's philosophical writings, but do not influence their validity one way or another.

The articles in the *Magazin* as well as his stand for Haeckel, the evolutionary biologist, and for Nietzsche and his new morality show Steiner consistently on the side of the progressives. His perception had always told him that a conservative and dogmatic church stood in the way of truth. The scientific method was in his opinion capable of refinement so that it could overcome the materialism inherent in its more primitive stages. His concern was with the development of this method. Why should it not be able to do justice to the phenomena of growing and dying, to the full range of human emotions and to man's perception of spirituality? There was no need to succumb to the easy way out of the reductionists who simply declare any approach 'pre-scientific' which is likely to upset their arbitrarily appointed boundaries. Steiner believed in development, in the sense of considering not only what is, but also what could come into existence. His outlook was essentially evolutionary and he felt that just as Darwin had made the evolutionary outlook acceptable in academic circles so Haeckel was making it acceptable to the general public of Central Europe.

The same progressive attitude Steiner also showed towards Nietzsche. He was well aware that Darwinism through its stress on the struggle for existence can lead to a gross materialism and brutalism, both of which he abhorred. Equally he must have been aware of the tenuous border between Nietzsche and the extreme Right, the advocates of naked power. In his *Philosophy of Freedom* he is as radical as Nietzsche, but also very sensitive to the social implications of moral individualism.

The Philosophy of Freedom was written in Weimar. The work consists of two parts, the first dealing with the reality of the act of thinking, the second of an approach to ethics in which the idea of 'thou shalt' is wholy absent. Too often the first part is considered as something in itself, but this is not what Steiner intended. In a lecture[5] given in 1918 when the book came out in a new edition he said: "I wrote" it "in order to put before mankind clearly and simply the idea, the impulse of freedom." He based this idea on the philosophical outlook which had already become manifest in the works mentioned earlier. These considerations form the first part 'The Science of Freedom', and are followed by 'The Reality of Freedom' which describes the free man aware of his position as a unique centre in which all the forces of the universe come into play; how such a man can live up to his responsibility and how in a world of free men cooperation is achieved. "Living in the love of action and letting live in the understanding of the impulses of others". 'Freedom' by itself and taken to extremes can lead to terrorism. The sensitive awareness of 'The Reality of Freedom' is meant to prevent this.

Some General Remarks

The aim of the next two chapters is to present the reader with an account of some of the essential insights which Steiner articulated in his teaching. The reader is asked not to expect a summary of Steiner's views or a potted version of his thoughts, but an attempt to state in contemporary terms some facts which are basic to Steiner's teaching and which he expressed as befitted his audiences of two or three generations ago. It is an attempt which Steiner expected from his pupils. He indicated to the teachers of the Waldorfschule his wish that they should rewrite his basic books for those born around 1910, something which has hardly been done so far. Nor will it be done here because we are not following the design of any particular work of Steiner's, nor are we attempting a comprehensive account of his whole opus, a task beyond the possibilities of the present writer. But it is hoped that as a result of these two chapters many a reader will be encouraged to study Steiner's works themselves. Suggestions of how to proceed with such a study will be found in Chapter Ten.

Steiner's place as a spiritual *teacher* is unique, not only because of *what* he taught, but also because of the *way* he presented his facts. He speaks of a *science* of the spirit and he often calls this 'science'

Anthroposophy. What he means by 'science' is a question of attitude, of tone and style. He avoids generalities, he avoids sentimentality. He points to distinct, concrete facts within the totality of phenomena experienced by men. We find the same abrupt change with which in the realm of philosophical discussion Socrates confronted his contemporaries. The older philosophers had started with propositions as "Being is (exists), non-being is not (does not exist), or 'War is the father of all things'. Socrates encouraged his friends to observe how the cobbler works or what good scratching does. Of course, people were shocked.

This shock is felt even more in the case of a spiritual teacher. He ought, people feel, to speak in religious or mystical terms and concern himself with statements of a general and all-embracing nature. To them Steiner is shockingly concrete and cold. They look at him with as much mistrust as Socrates was looked at by those who were familiar with earlier forms of philosophy.

By calling his teaching Anthroposophy he wanted to emphasise, among other things, that the study of man, provided that it deals with the totality of observable phenomena, is capable of throwing light on many of our most profound questions concerning the nature of man as well as the nature of the universe. So it seems, at least initially, surprising that he called his first basic book *Theosophy*, and that he kept this title in editions published after his break with the Theosophical Society. But the title is correct. In this book Steiner articulates in an entirely modern manner what theosophical and spiritual wisdom had taught throughout the ages: the intimate connection of man, earth and cosmos, man's cosmic origin and his many-layered nature. We shall treat this part of Steiner's teaching under the title of *Universe, Earth and Man*, a title which he chose for one of his lecture courses.[6] A second part will be called *Christ and the Destiny of Man*. There we shall speak about those aspects of Steiner's teaching which concern the future of earth and man, and man's destiny, aspects deeply imbued with Steiner's experience of Christ and thereby entirely different from ancient, especially Eastern wisdom.

The fact that Steiner spoke about distinct, concrete facts enabled his followers to build up many activities based on his insights. We shall discuss them in the chapters on Social and Cultural Initiatives. These activities owe a great deal to the discipline which Steiner had laid upon himself. Asked by a spiritually advanced woman whether there were any contemporary initiates able to penetrate as widely and as far as he, he is reported to have said: "Yes, indeed. But there is nobody else capable of putting his visions into thoughts so that others are able to think these thoughts themselves and thereby experience them. This presupposes carrying the experiences of spiritual vision right into the brain and this is a sacrifice of which others are incapable.[7]

Chapter Four
Universe, Earth and Man

Natural Science and the Science of the Spirit

Steiner approved of the method of natural science in his day, but he insisted that science had adopted, quite arbitrarily, a set of blinkers and therefore refused to consider the *totality* of known phenomena – and even more the possibility that beyond the limits of its arbitrarily drawn borders other fields might lie which could provide essential insights into our nature and the world within which we have our existence. He further insisted that there was a need constantly to review the philosophical and sociological bases of science and to state exactly what was theory, model, habit of thinking or unchallenged fact.

To give one example: We were all educated to believe that the 'struggle for existence' and the 'survival of the fittest' were facts deduced from nature and were the only explanation available. In fact, Darwin borrowed these two terms from Malthus. This clergyman observed the devastating social consequences of the Industrial Revolution in rural England and came up with a theory designed to assuage the bad conscience of his richer parishioners and to save them from giving alms. In other words: The brutal behaviour of Englishmen of 160 years ago was superimposed on facts which had been observed by Darwin and proclaimed as a 'law'. However, there are facts which give us an entirely different picture. The lion cannot exist without gazelles, but gazelles depend on lions as well. Without these lions the gazelles as a species would deteriorate and finally die out. Inferior stock would live and mate. An overabundance of gazelles would destroy the grass cover of the savannah. As it is, grass, gazelles and lions co-exist. There is a natural ecological balance.

Whether we lay stress on this balance or on the struggle for existence will have far-reaching consequences. If this struggle were an objective fact and contradicted by no other facts, aggression and unlimited competition would only be 'natural'. We then could be brutal while feeling smug in the knowledge that we are simply behaving as creatures of nature 'red in tooth and claw'. Somehow, this view has penetrated our society, but it is not based on an appreciation of the *totality* of observable facts.

The scientific establishment, furthermore decides which studies are to be pursued and which not. Homoeopathy, Freudian and Jungian psychology met with extraordinary resistance and even today are often allowed but a peripheral existence. In the United States there is a fierce battle for positions in academic and industrial life between Behaviourists and Freudians, who are, however, united in keeping out the disciples of, say, Victor Frankl. This means in practice that the more narrow-mindedly mechanistic a person's outlook is, the more likely he is to acquire a position of power and responsibility. For the academic establishment is largely financed by the military-industrial complex whose interest lies in the manipulation of nature, and who are not known to be much interested in the inner dimension of existence. The result is that almost universally *opinions* are given out as established *fact;* we are lulled into the belief that we have satisfactory answers to all the major questions, and that what we do not know today is hardly worth knowing.

Maya

Over thousands of years a consensus of great thinkers have come to the opposite view: The inner world is more 'real' and true than the evidence of our senses. The world of the senses is a great illusion, is *maya*. Steiner holds with Goethe that, rightly approached, the sense world can teach us a great many important things, and that we learn more if we approach it in terms of processes, of polarities, of metamorphosis rather than as an odd assembly of pieces of dead matter. One of the most important processes which we can easily observe and contemplate is our breathing. It never ceases from the moment we are born to the moment of our death. It pulsates, it has a rhythmic quality. There is a constant interplay between contraction (systole) and expansion (diastole). The act of breathing out leads quite spontaneously to its opposite, to breathing in. At the one extreme our breath mingles with the air outside and is largely indistinguishable from it, at the other extreme it appears to be our very own, our private property.

The reader familiar with oriental thinking will detect here the Chinese polarity of *yin* and *yang*. Steiner frequently speaks about breathing, he describes it in its observable and concrete details, where the Chinese sage starts with a cosmic principle. The present writer knows of no particular passage where Steiner looks at breathing as a general principle, but when describing other phenomena he frequently treats them in a similar manner. He speaks about the polarities of day and night, of waking and sleeping consciousness, of winter and summer, of life and death and he looks at their rhythmic quality, their systole and diastole. If we adopt his attitude and learn to appreciate the world and its phenomena in terms of processes which we understand because we can both experience and study them, our whole attitude to the world around us and our place in it will change. Imperceptibly, the illusion of a cold, hostile unchanging world out there will give way to something profound and 'true'. The maya character will be lessened, the world will become an interplay of powerful processes, it will become mobile, approachable, woven out of the substance and manifesting the processes which sustain us as well. A first step is made towards man-within-nature, of man-within-the-universe.

Man's Cosmic Origin

No philosopher or scientist, mystic or seer has been able to give us a verifiable account of the origin of the world, of the origin of substance or of the origin of life. Nor has Steiner. We simply cannot conceive that we fallible men could imagine how a universe of such super-human magnitude has come about. The materialist cannot go beyond some hypothetical primal matter which, according to one recently current theory, produced a 'big bang'. Such a theory presupposes the existence of energy and matter. The religious man cannot answer the familiar question of 'who made God?'. He does not have to either, for his definition of God includes the notion that He created Himself.

But one thing is certain: We are living in a mysterious universe, and it is a major loss of our civilisation that everything is done to gloss over this awesome fact. Steiner does not indulge in speculations about the origin of the universe, but gives a pre-history of the earth and man which leads us back to the birth moment of the earth, man and the solar system. In this far-distant epoch spiritual beings of various magnitudes already existed.

The account which Steiner gives of subsequent events is best read in *Occult Science'*, an account which is factual and 'objective'. Another account is given in a course of lectures[1] where he mainly speaks of the

Beings who brought about the whole development. If we leave out the details – though they are often of immense profundity – we arrive at certain basic ideas which can be imagined by many people and which to some carry the unmistakable ring of truth.

The process which culminated in the existence of our earth took aeons of time and was not accomplished all at once. The present author imagines this process as one of cosmic breathing. An outbreathing took place which created 'physical substance' in its most sublimated form. Steiner describes this world in terms of our present earthly understanding as a universe of warmth in rich differentiation. Then this 'outer' universe came to an end. A cosmic inbreathing took place and the first forerunner of our earth was internalised into the world of cosmic beings. A second and a third stage followed in which the outbreathing resulted in successively denser and more material states: first the gaseous and then the fluid state was achieved. Then, after the third inbreathing, came what we now know as our planet, the earth. It did not start with solid matter, but through a process of densification repeated, more quickly, the previous planetary states until solid matter crystallised and dense substance was at last achieved.

Closely bound up with this evolution went the development of man, who at every stage acquired more power, diversity and identity. Today, we experience ourselves and our fellow men as many-layered beings, full of hidden depths and contradictions, but also with an unfathomable potential for further development. Steiner never wearies of pointing to the immense complexity of man and opening up ever more profound secrets, many of which we are able to verify even without having ourselves the perception of the clairvoyant. This process of verification is essential for the anthroposophist who is bidden to avoid *believing* what Steiner has to tell him. Some parts of this teaching appear self-evident; others can be verified by an increased sensitivity in observing ourselves, as well as others; while some parts can be understood as soon as we have learned to look in a qualitative way at natural processes within man and outside. The complexity of man is so great that even in *Theosophy*, his first book on these matters, Steiner describes the human being in four different ways, as a threefold being and as a fourfold, sevenfold and ninefold entity. We shall now turn to the first and second of these endeavours to describe adequately human nature in its fullness.

Body, Soul and Spirit

The division of the complete human being into three qualitatively very different modes of experience can be expressed in well-known, though sometimes ill-defined terms.

Our 'body' is the basis of our earthly existence. With its incredibly differentiated organs, senses, muscles, brain, liver, etc., it is able to perform extremely complicated and diverse processes such as seeing, breathing, digesting. Without it we would have no sense impressions, no emotions, no awareness of our existence. But this need not blind us to the fact that there are two other areas of our being which have a fundamentally different quality.

There is the world of our psychological personality. It is a world of emotions. It is a world of internalisation. There is for example, a fundamental difference between the sense impression of the sea at Land's End and the memory of it which suddenly arises in me, out of nowhere as it seems. Such a memory need not be paler than the original sense impression, in certain circumstances it can be more colourful, more strongly imbued with meaning, more dynamic and powerful. The details may have changed and the significant parts stand out in greater clarity. A process of metamorphosis and internalisation has taken place, a process which cannot be described in terms of the 'body'. In Steiner's terminology it belongs to the realm of the soul.

Such distinctions should be clearly seen, particularly as many scientists feel obliged to obliterate the utterly different quality of body and soul owing to their determination to allow nothing unless it is causally determined and can be explained in mechanistic terms. C. G. Jung is one of those who fully recognise the difference between body and what he calls 'psyche'. The reductionist on the other hand, will point out to us that there is no difference: he can cause definite and foreseeable emotions simply by the stimulation of certain nerve ends in the brain. What he is unlikely to tell us, however, is that the person so stimulated experiences the emotion as something foreign to him. He will feel, say, fear, but wonder why on earth he should have felt fear when there was nothing to frighten him and he himself was not in a fearful state. The experimenter manages to get at the bodily basis of an emotional experience, but can produce only a surrogate which the person concerned can easily distinguish from the real thing. The unique flavour of the soul experience, its internalised quality has not been achieved; the realm of the soul has not been entered.

When today we use the words 'spirit' or 'spiritual' we often think of something vague, pleasant and good. Steiner's use of the word 'spirit' is much more precise. Over a long period of time we have stopped observing and contemplating phenomena which have a spiritual quality in Steiner's sense of the term. So we must now proceed gradually. Steiner advises us to observe the process of thinking. This is another world of internalisation, but is obviously not charged with emotion. We cannot clearly and logically think if we are swamped by joy, passion, fear – though in such situations we may experience a new insight, a sudden intuition. The process of thinking needs calm detachment. Although it appears to happen within the privacy of our self it is, if properly carried through, objective. It can be fully communicated to others; they can go through exactly the same process, and arrive at the same result. This is obviously not the case with soul experiences. I can only partly communicate to others my experience of yesterday's sunset and nobody can experience it exactly in the way I did, whether he stood at my side when the event happened or whether he was subsequently given an account of my impressions and sensations.

We have now arrived at a third field of experience, that of the spirit: a non-corporeal, calm, objective world which for him who becomes familiar with its working holds experiences as rich as does the soul world. Predictably, the reductionist will point out that thinking is nothing but certain electrical impulses in our brain. He is wrong. Again he mistakes the physical basis, the instrument, with the process, the tune played on this instrument. Moritz Schlick, the great logical positivist and founder of the Vienna Circle used to say: "If somebody tells me that two and two makes five I shall not send him to a brain surgeon for an operation, but I shall argue with him."

Observation of the process of thinking can teach us important lessons about ourselves and can help us understand as a first step what Steiner meant by 'spirit'. Without doubt we are the producers of our thought. But the thoughts so produced do not speak about our individuality, as our soul experiences do, but make a statement about the world. They complement the world of objects. On its own a rosebush in flower is a meaningless, though pleasant, phenomenon. The rosebush receives meaning through my thoughts, – thoughts about the appearance of the bush in the different seasons of the year, about wild and cultivated roses, other rosaceae, etc. Through thinking I begin for the first time to appreciate the unique character of the rose, its relation to climate and soil, its history. My senses simply presented me with a particular bush at a particular moment of its development. Together, the evidence of the senses and the result of my thinking establish the *meaningful reality*. My thought activity, a spiritual process in Steiner's terms, has given me a first understanding of the spiritual aspect of the world, the meaning of its existence.

The clear distinction of the respective qualities of body, soul and spirit can also be grasped in different and slightly easier ways. As Steiner developed his teaching he found it increasingly useful to speak about the three soul faculties of thinking, feeling and willing with their obvious relations to spirit, soul and body, and about three interpenetrating systems of the body, nerves and senses centred in the head, breathing and blood circulation centred in the middle, and the metabolic system connected to abdomen and limbs. But body, soul and spirit have also much wider connotations and it is to these that we now turn. They are, however, best approached if we look at Steiner's presentation of man as a fourfold being.

The Four Bodies

If Steiner speaks of four bodies which each of us is supposed to have it is obvious that for him the term 'body' has a different meaning than for most other people. We have already seen that he is more aware of processes than of solid substances. That this is a helpful and realistic approach can be seen if we ask people what they understand by 'earth', the globe which is our home. Most people would instinctively visualise the ground under their feet. But at sea level our planet consists of vastly more water than solid rock. Our bias towards solid substance gives us therefore a distorted picture of what our globe in reality is.

Body, for Steiner, is a delicately structured organism the constituents of which are part of a much greater whole. Our body, in Steiner's language our *physical* body, obviously consists of materials taken from the earth: the calcium in our bones, the silicon of our hair, the oxygen and nitrogen in our lungs, the blood, possibly the water of the primeval ocean, we borrow these and all other substances for the duration of this life. Similarly, Steiner explains, we have in addition an *etheric* body, a highly differentiated field of formative forces which in different (though related) ways plants and animals also possess. Then there is the *astral* body which only animals and men have.

These 'bodies' are not easily visualised unless we learn to 'see' them clairvoyantly. But anthroposophical scientists, doctors and farmers work with those etheric forces in man, nature and cosmos, and a number of techniques have been established to show – not these forces themselves, which by definition are not physical – but the consequences of their activity in earthly substances. When Steiner speaks about *astrality* he means to convey that superpersonal, cosmic forces are interwoven into our emotional being. This is not so far removed from what many contemporaries have learned from depth psychology: the intensely dynamic quality of our emotions and the fact that these emotions can be experienced as an autonomous region, which is quite often outside our control. Notwithstanding our personal differences, our emotional life – our astrality in Steiner's terminology – has many features which are universal to man.

The fourth 'body' Steiner calls the Ego or I. It is the most difficult to approach. Steiner describes this Ego as the true centre of man and the other three 'bodies' as sheaths which envelop and house it. Unfortunately, many people influenced by Eastern thought look today at the term Ego as something egotistical and unspiritual. We shall see in the next chapter how strongly Steiner differs from the East just in this respect. For the moment we can suggest that the Ego might be looked at as a seed of immense potential for growth and development. Steiner very carefully points out that the Ego is the least developed of the four bodies, but that the future of the individual as well as of the totality of man depends on the use made of this Ego. Steiner's term comprises Jung's two terms of Ego, with its negative connotations, and Self, seen as good, but goes beyond it. Through contemplation and meditative practice we can develop our Ego from its egotistical beginnings to a true evaluation of our being and from there to an awareness of the Divinity in us. The way forward lies for Steiner in an ever-increasing self knowledge, in laying bare the three sheaths and in grounding ourselves in man's eternal part, his Ego. This process leads to an ever-growing awareness of those regions of our being which are spiritual, sublime and divine.

A Provisional Summary

Steiner expresses, in largely new terms, a view of life that has been held over the whole globe throughout the ages; that man, earth and universe are made of the same stuff. From this it follows that there must be essential connections between the three, and in his work Steiner draws attention to many of these. But the origin of all is Being, which appears in many forms down to lifeless matter. "Substance is the end of the ways of God", a Christian thinker of a former age tells us. Steiner also endeavours to tell us of the incredible complexity of the human being which shows features that connect it with the world of minerals, with plants, with animals and with the Divine, – a being which at one pole, is driven by his unconscious, the will in Steiner's terminology, and which, at the other, can delight in the spiritual activities of thinking and meditating.

Chapter Five
Christ and the Destiny of Man

During his years in Weimar and Berlin Steiner made not a few remarks which indicate a cool, even hostile attitude to Christianity and, sometimes, to religion as such. He wrote to Rosa Mayreder[1] that man has the right to create and that his creation has the same right to existence as anything else. But men are weak. Instead of proudly acknowledging their creativity in the spiritual realm they claim it all comes from their Father in Heaven. Too frightened to *wollen* (to live out their impulse) they pretend to *sollen* (to be compelled to). But in the very same year he puts his basic awareness of the free human being also in a context which assumes the existence of the Divine.[2] God – he does not use His name, but speaks of 'the highest potency of existence' – in infinite love has given Himself to reappear within man, and to work acts of freedom. Once man becomes aware of this fact he will revolt against any 'pseudo-God', a tyrant outside himself. Three years later he identifies with Nietzsche's attacks on Christianity in his *Antichrist*. "In every sentence I found my own emotions expressed."[3]

At first, such remarks seem puzzling, but there are a number of explanations which might help towards an understanding. We have stressed that from his very beginnings Steiner experienced the *totality* of the world of matter and of mind. His very being had to be in revolt against a dualistic interpretation of this totality, particularly when a power-seeking church stood behind it, a church which purported to know in every detail what God's commandments were and thereby held men in thrall. This ran counter to another of Steiner's basic experiences, the absolute awareness of the potential of freedom in man. On the other hand, what Schuré reported might be true also in this respect and Steiner might have immersed himself completely in materialism in order to gain from this experience. (See *Three Encounters*.) Or he might even have felt the heavy burden of his early clairvoyance and tried to rid himself of it, – though there are only a very few indications that this might have been so.

A Festival of Knowledge

However, events took a different turn, one apparently completely unexpected by Steiner himself. He had an overwhelming spiritual experience which, to the best of this writer's knowledge, he described but once.[4] It was his Damascus. The experience probably lasted a considerable time and concerned what Steiner came to call the Mystery of Golgotha, the passion, death and resurrection of Christ. What tradition and the rites of the church had been unable to give him was now granted to him in what he described as an *Erkenntnisfeier*, a solemn festival of actively gaining insight of immense depth and width. The light of this experience dispelled any doubts, confirmed his deep awareness of the free man, of the unity of the physical and spiritual aspects of reality, and of the evolutionary principle. It opened up a new future for him, provided there were people who out of their deepest longing freely wished to share his newly-found Christian vision.

There are not a few people who on their approach to Anthroposophy are shocked to find that in the centre of Steiner's teaching stands the figure of the Christ. Others who in their childhood have not experienced the narrow orthodoxies or sentimental generalities which all too often are taken as Christ's teaching feel an immediate onrush of joy at the profound spirituality which pervades everything that Steiner has to say about the life, deeds and impulses of Christ. Here lies indeed the heart of Steiner's teaching in which Christ is the main character Whose light illumines everything.[5]

A man steeped in the traditions of historical Christianity will soon notice an apparent, but glaring contradiction. When standing before the great events in Palestine Steiner will make no concessions to the theology of the last centuries. Like Paul he insists that if the Resurrection was not a fact, all talk of Christianity is vain. What in the past the churches used to teach is here put into a modern and spiritual context which enables us to approach emotionally and with deep understanding what at first seemed miraculous and incredible. But as soon as Steiner turns to the consequences of Christ's deeds for our moral and spiritual being he is poles apart from the churches. We are not told what we ought to do on the basis of God's commandments – be they authentic, or a convenient way of keeping people in a state of dependence; but we are helped on our way to self awareness and social interaction. We feel liberated and ennobled, new virtues arise in us and old ones deepen: compassion, independence of judgement, personal responsibility, social and ecological awareness. We begin to feel totally responsible for our own future, for the future of mankind and of the earth.

The Fifth Gospel

The gospels report Christ's promise that He will be with us to the end of the earth's history. Throughout the last 2000 years many people have, often with great surprise, confirmed the truth of this promise. He has been *experienced* as a giver of insights, as a teacher. Some of these insights changed the face of Christianity, others lived on only in small communities. Steiner was certain that Christ's revelation is an ongoing process which will continue to 'the end of the days' and that he himself stood within this process ever since the event referred to on the previous page. He was, however, far from claiming that this had been the final insight. "It will be necessary to throw light on ever new aspects of this greatest mystery in man's earthly evolution in order only approximately to approach from the most diverse sides the Mystery of Golgotha"[6]. "For Christ stands before us not like one fully dead, but fully alive and what He has to give us can be experienced always anew by those whose spiritual eyes are opened."[7]

So we can speak of a continuing revelation of Christ, the Fifth Gospel, and Steiner does not hesitate to give detailed and concrete descriptions of events in the life of Jesus which the gospels do not mention. But equally arresting are also the explanations of those events which have been familiar to Christians through the centuries, the Temptation, the Transfiguration, the Ascension, etc. Some of these events were previously described as 'miracles', that is as unique and inexplicable interferences in a mechanical universe. But once we have understood that the very nature of our universe is spiritual such events remain still unique, but in tune with the very core of all existence. These miracles, – Steiner prefers to call them tokens – become in such a context totally removed from the world of the conjuror and magician and are revealed in their full profundity, as events in the world of spiritual powers and principalities of which we ordinary men are vouchsafed the occasional glimpse and to which we can therefore feel related.

The World in Evolution

Christian thinkers in contrast to Eastern sages are used to looking at human history as a tremendous dramatic process characterised by events such as the Fall, the Incarnation, the Judgement. But essentially their outlook had also static qualities, particularly where the divine world was concerned. There are no changes in eternity. Steiner is probably the first Christian thinker who fully accepted the reality of the evolutionary process. Nature, human consciousness, the relation of man to his spiritual origin, even the world of Divine Beings is changing and evolving.

In a vast number of lectures Steiner attempted to arouse in his audience an awareness of the diversity of human experience. We have totally different expectations and frames of reference from Englishmen of only two generations ago, we experience different things, overlook what was important to them, use our senses differently, in brief, our lives have an utterly different quality from theirs. No longer do we presume that our culture is the only one which matters and others are to be measured by the degree of similarity to European standards. We recognise the validity of any culture and have respect for their otherness. So Steiner's insistence on the changing human consciousness does not sound so strange to us as it did to most of his contemporaries. Man embedded in the universe, in his family, in his nation has given way to the lonely individual, to alienated man. We often look back with nostalgic longing to those older forms of consciousness without realising that our loss was also our gain. In this tragic process we gained our independence, our self-reliance, our individuality, our freedom.

Early man – we can study his mind in innumerable myths and stories – was no stranger in the world. He lived in a world of blurred boundaries. God, demigod, hero, man was but a gradation of existence. Man, animals, clouds, water, plants, earth belonged to *one* community. Life and death, birth and death were not polar opposites, they were part of an eternal rhythm. But gradually the lines of distinction began to stand out. Just as the small child experiences a shrinking of consciousness – "this is *not* I" is what the world around is constantly teaching him – so the consciousness of mankind shrank and became more clearly focussed. But the world around ceased to speak. It became dead. The creator beings were no longer experienced and, later, men were not even aware of those traces in nature which revealed the handiwork of these creative powers. The world became mechanical and dull. A tragic situation. For if this process were to continue unchecked the result could only be total alienation, despair, aggression, death.

Father and Son

This was the situation which Christ came to redeem, – though we shall see later that this is not the only aspect which we have to appreciate. The Divine Son entered the world of man, the world of despair, betrayal, death. What divine beings had never experienced, death, Christ faced in its most terrifying, sickening form. Until then man had experienced the majesty of the Creator, the Ground of the World, the Father. They had revered and adored Him. They knew awe. They experienced the descending and ascending chain of beings which led them far beyond the realm of man into hierarchical worlds and into the womb of the Creative Mother or Father. In their earthly affairs this experience was mirrored. Below their ruler, the 'son of heaven', the 'living god' spread out a hierarchical order in which each man had his God-given place.

But the Son entered the world of the children of God as our brother. He lay in the manger, He learned a trade, He came to experience misunderstanding, hatred, betrayal, loneliness, agony. He spoke and listened to fishermen and tax collectors, to sinners and outcasts, the soldiers of the occupying power more than to priests, kings and scholars. There was no hierarchical order, there was no remoteness. The people around Christ experienced a presence of Divine spirituality which simply had invaded the world of their daily lives. Directly, and at their own level they were aware of God. He faced them as their equal and yet time and again they were overwhelmed by His power, His understanding and His sublimity. A new realm had become manifest which did not cancel the realm of the Father, but clearly and distinctly co-existed with it. It reached its full majesty in the Mystery of Golgotha.

Rudolf Steiner – possibly as nobody before him – makes a qualitative distinction between God the Father and God the Son without, of course, denying their identity. "I and the Father are One" is for Steiner not only a fact, but also a guiding word for all striving men. But it is obvious that the mystery of God's threefold manifestation is not one that can be neatly analysed and logically resolved. It can, however, in Wittgenstein's terminology, be 'pointed at' and clearly experienced.

Jesus and Christ

A quite different distinction is more readily understood. It is the distinction between the man Jesus of Nazareth and the God that dwelt within him, the Christ. The Eastern churches call the time up to Christ's coming to earth 'God becoming Man'. What this means concretely is shown by Steiner from many aspects and in great detail. The process of incarnation, a shrinking, a densification into physical substance stretches over a vast amount of time. We can learn to appreciate some of these descending steps into a human body. We also learn to understand how men in widely different cultures were able to experience the approach of the Divine Son, the Incarnating Logos, the Cosmic Word. Two cultures experienced and understood this approach more clearly than any others: the Greeks and the Jews.

Also a body had to be prepared which could be the dwelling place of the God. Infinite wisdom was necessary, wisdom far beyond human intelligence, to distil the substance, physical, etheric and astral, which could be the vehicle of Christ. This process culminated in the twelfth year of Jesus of Nazareth. Eighteen years later, at the baptism in the Jordan, the Christ could enter this body and dwell there for the next two and a quarter years. – Anthroposophists usually call this period the Three Years. – These years witnessed the final stages of the descent, a further shrinking which caused ineffable suffering, partly by the Son's recognition of the human condition, man's frailty, man's tragedy, sorrow and despair, and partly by the ever more complete identification with the earthly man Jesus and his crumbling body. At the beginning of the three years there was often manifest the superhuman power of the Christ, at the end there was the despair and cold sweat in the garden of Gethsemane.

The Turning Point of Time

During the last centuries an understanding of the spiritual implications of Christ's resurrection has grown dimmer. So people focussed their interest on what Christ *said*. Steiner's first concern is with what Christ *did*. However beautiful and profound his sayings are, they are still but a 'pointing' to an existential fact, the fact that the Divine Son appeared in the sense world in which he acted and suffered openly and publicly. The consequences of His deeds are described by Steiner as objective facts which brought about the greatest change in direction in the evolution of man, a change which according to Steiner happened within man as well as within the body of our planet.

It is not difficult to see what he meant as far as the subsequent history of mankind is concerned. In pre-Christian times two ideas of time were prevalent: the cyclical aspect of time, the view that there is a regular rhythm of up and down turns with the result that overall nothing changes, and the experience of the decline of mankind, the change from a paradisal golden age to a silver age, a bronze age and finally to the harsh iron age, our own.

All this changed with the coming of Christianity. The Christian bible begins with the creation and paradise and ends with the heavenly Jerusalem. The first image put before us is that of the Garden, full of innocence and abundant with life, God-given and whole. At the end stands the image of the City, man-made, resplendent, redeemed, man again united with God, the creation restored to its full splendour and enriched by an unfathomable wealth of experience. In other words, there is meaning in the history of the earth and this meaning is given us through Christ's deeds. In the ninth century John Scotus Erigena saw an evolution in three steps: the revelation of the Father accompanied by the ten commandments and the Mosaic priesthood, followed by the revelation of the Son with his message of love, and the Christian priesthood. This will be superseded by the revelation of the Spirit. Then we shall act out of our own insights and each man will be a priest. Similar optimistic views were proclaimed in the twelfth century by Joaquim a Fiore. It is only through what Steiner calls the Christ impulse that the belief has arisen that whatever our present difficulties and crises the best times lie ahead of us. This conviction provided a spur and helped to forge the belief in the inexorable course of progress which characterised our modern technological civilisation, a belief which only in the last decade or two has been seriously questioned. It is this dynamism and optimism of Christianity which can help to explain some puzzling historical facts. How could the inhabitants of the smallest continent spread their culture over the whole globe and settle down in so many parts of it? How was it possible for these Europeans to surpass the intellectual, scientific and technological achievements of the Chinese who for thousands of years had been in the vanguard of development?

It is not so easy to see the change in man which the Mystery of Golgotha brought about but it can be experienced by ordinary people of our age. Christ brought with Him and put at man's disposal the realm of the Son, which allows us to develop a new spirituality, social awareness and ecological responsibility, while experiencing at the same time the Realm of the Father with its totally different quality. But it is impossible for the non-clairvoyant man to test Steiner's statements concerning the effects of the Mystery of Golgotha on the body of the earth. He repeatedly and emphatically asserted that there were definite changes in the hard structure of our planet and that today in particular the airy regions of the earth are permeated by the substance of the Resurrected.

The Ego: Freedom and Love

In the previous chapter we referred to Steiner's teaching of the Ego. Eastern wisdom sees in this Ego the source of man's sufferings and illusions, Steiner knows that a man who consciously confronts his unique existence stands at the beginning of a process of spiritual growth. For this Ego is God-given and is of His substance. When Moses asked God to reveal His identity the reply given was: I am the *I am*. The awareness of Being, of Eternity in us whether gained through sudden enlightenment or through disciplined and faithful meditation over a period of time reveals a Divine kernel within us which consciously used can transform ourselves and the world. What to Moses was a revelation from beyond became in Christ's ministry upon earth an inner experience of those around Him. They experienced an overabundance of love streaming towards them from the very centre of their teacher and they found themselves raised into a realm of freedom unknown to them before. But at the same time they learned to ennoble that part of their being which came neither from father nor from mother, but was found as the unique centre of their being, the seed implanted by the Father and invigorated and brought to life by the Son. Tribal man knows love as a natural instinct, many a mother is surprised by the unexpected upwelling of love for her new-born babe. The love of which Christ speaks is the love of the free, even the alienated man. It is the outpouring and sharing of a man's spirituality kindled by compassion and a recognition of the other's spiritual identity, his Ego.

So we come to the essence of Christ's teaching, the interplay of love and freedom. Each of these in isolation can lead to excess and perversion. In harmony with each other they transform our existence and redeem the world. Many a great Christian of previous ages became aware of these facts through his contemplation of Christ. However, on the large, universal scale we may very well feel that Christianity has not failed, it has hardly ever been tried. Then we may wonder whether it is not up to us to help form the new world based on the recognition of man's spiritual nature and Christ's deed, an Ego-filled responsibility, compassion, love and freedom. If we are inclined to make an attempt at the 'New World' it might be best to look first at the hindrances, at man's potential for evil. But even before this exercise I would ask myself: Can what Steiner has said be true?

Too Beautiful to be True?

Steiner encouraged us to question and test his teaching. Does it agree with observed facts? Is it contradicting itself? How does it relate to our own common sense and inborn feeling for truth? But he put his Christian teaching in a different category. If the Mystery of Golgotha could be proved logically or factually it would straight-away lose its meaning. It lies outside the realm of causality, it is a free deed, the greatest possible free deed.[8]

We cannot argue about Christ's deed, but we can experience our relationship to Him. Such a relationship can be started by either side. We know of plenty of cases in Christian history where a man suddenly was overwhelmed by the unexpected presence of Christ. But equally, we too can start this relationship. As an entirely free deed we begin to grope towards Him and wait quietly for what may happen. We put ourselves at risk, just as a lover puts himself at risk if there is no initial response to his love. But without taking this risk we cannot grow. Suppose, we fail to find anything of interest in great music. We then may say 'boring' and leave it at that. But, perhaps encouraged by some friend we may grope forward in the hope that meaning and joy might be discovered in what seemed simply repetitive noises. Joy and meaning might be found, but they also might not. Similarly with Christ. He cannot be forced, but He can be loved in freedom.

All through history, Steiner felt, there were people who did not simply believe in Christ, think about Him, but genuinely met Him.

Some met Him totally unexpectedly, others established a relationship through their imaginative understanding of the gospels, others through their experience during the Mass in its various forms, others through their patient contemplation and meditation. All these ways are still open to modern man. But he has two more ways as well. He can contemplate those insights given him by that great disciple of Christ, Rudolf Steiner. He can also experience Him through his social relationships. It is this aspect which Steiner towards the end of his life dwells on more and more. "Where two or three are gathered together in Christ's name" has been an overwhelming experience for Steiner and for not a few of his students. Through this stress on the Christian character of inter-personal relationships and on the total lack of compulsion Steiner can be felt to have interesting similarities with a remarkable strand in the religious and cultural life of England. Similar perceptions inspired some of the more radical sects in the 1640s and were kept alive to the present day in the Society of Friends.[9] Steiner's perception, however, may strike us as more spiritual and profound and at the same time thoroughly modern.

Karma

While Steiner dropped many Indian terms which he had used at the beginning of the century he used the word *Karma* to the end of his life. The number of people familiar with this term and its traditional meaning was small at that time, and so Steiner was able to use it in a particular sense which would have been more difficult had he used *Schicksal,* the word available in the German language for *destiny* and *fate*. But today, when Indian terminology lives much more strongly in the minds of Westerners, it is necessary to make clear at the outset that in Steiner's mouth the word *Karma* carries connotations and undertones quite different from the traditional Eastern usage. In brief, Steiner transposes the word from the realm of the Father to the realm of the Son, from an iron law as unchangeable as the laws of nature to a network of relationships in the world of compassion, freedom and love.

Human Fallibility

Each one of us is aware of his own imperfections. Every week we do things which we bitterly regret afterwards and which we know we *could* have done better. But also on a larger scale we know, we are not the men we *could* be. There lives in us a sense of non-fulfilment, of imperfection which obviously causes tension. But we can also look at our fallibility as the greatest glory of the human race. The animal is, to use a modern expression, perfectly programmed. In its natural habitat it makes no mistake. It is part of nature. As we have seen before, early man was also part of nature and stepped out of it only very gradually and painfully. Most mythologies have amusing stories about the first liar and trickster. The first lie was a human achievement. A man had stepped out of nature and now had to take responsibility for what he had said and done. The first step into freedom was made and for the first time the question of morality arose. Man had acquired the knowledge of good and evil.

The Question of Evil

Ever since, men have puzzled about the origin of evil. Theologians, philosophers, poets, sociologists have tried to unravel this mystery. Steiner's contribution is novel, profound and arresting, and forms an integral part of his Christian message as well as of his description of human psychology and development. Any human action or attitude *becomes* evil if it is displayed at the wrong place, the wrong time or in excess. Steiner, we know, believed in freedom, – in the sphere of morality, religion, cultural life, personal development, etc. But in economic life it leads to the immorality of capitalism, the ethics of the jungle, the absence of compassion. Or to take another and fairly unfashionable example: the free, self-motivating personality is the ideal of Steiner's art of education; but to set the child of three years 'free' is destructive. It deprives him of the ground under his feet and puts intolerable burdens on him. – The right impulse at the wrong time.

The second point which Steiner makes is that any attitude taken to excess is potentially evil. This means that Steiner does not think in terms of a simple polarity of good and evil, but for him good lies in the balance between two extremes, a balance which has to be newly achieved in every single instance. A simple example may illustrate the point. A child will be stunted if it has to grow up without the love of his parents or others who consciously take on the parents' role. But equally, an excessive amount of loving protection and concern will have a damaging effect leading to anxiety and dependence. The helpful attitude lies somewhere in the middle.

If evil lies in extreme attitudes, man has to face two different kinds of evil, – polar in character, but usually playing into each other's hands, one extreme generating the other as a response. The fact that men have an awareness of good and evil is due in the first place not to human psychology, but to man's cosmic development. Once man made the step into fallibility and into freedom moral tension became unavoidable. But his position became aggravated due to unequal development among superhuman entities in the spiritual hierarchies. Through the influence of certain of these powers, man made the fatal step too soon. His astrality, his emotional life, became overpowering, but at the same time he also acquired gifts, enthusiasm, a consciousness of himself, an urge for freedom. This mixed blessing – which few of us would now want to do without – was a gift of the being or beings whom Christians called Lucifer, the "Bearer of Light", who has been seen also as the Tempter and the Snake. He is then the 'warm and light-filled' extreme who inspires us, sets us aflame, wraps us up in a feeling of our own importance, encourages us to glory in our own being, makes us aware of our own spiritual potency, blinds us to the needs of our fellow men, destroys our connection to the demands of daily life on earth.

In turn, he stimulates his opposite, the 'dark and cold' power which Steiner, following Persian mythology calls Ahriman. He is the calculating manipulator who tries, not to seduce like Lucifer, but to enslave individual man, to make him part of a collective, to let him forget his cosmic origins, to chain him to a lifeless earth. If Ahriman had written a book making his claims clear he might easily have called it *Beyond Freedom and Dignity*. Aldous Huxley in *Brave New World* described graphically what a society dominated by Ahrimanic powers with the help of Luciferic dope might look like.

So man in his moral dilemma is placed into a struggle of cosmic powers far beyond human competence. Steiner repeatedly described the developments among the hierarchies which brought about this human predicament. But he teaches us also not to shun these powers or be frightened by them, but to accept what positive gifts they have to bestow on us, Lucifer's light-filled wisdom and urge for freedom, Ahriman's rationality and earthly know-how. To use their gifts without falling into the hands of these superhuman powers is a task beyond human strength. Therefore it was that Christ entered the evolution of the earth. Through Him we learn to use the urge towards freedom and the perfection of objective human intelligence so that they do not cause havoc to human development and human relationships. Through Him we learn to balance Lucifer and Ahriman, the left and the right side of our body. The achievement of this balance, the banishing of the two adversaries to their rightful places, the establishment of a space of freedom in which conscious and responsible man can work face to face with Christ is the subject of Steiner's great sculpture, the 'Group'.

This large wooden sculpture depicts the Representative of Man moving forward and bringing order and balance into the world of the two adversaries by directing them to those realms where their respective gifts can flourish without endangering man. The Representative of Man can be experienced as Christ, the God Incarnate, but also as the embodiment of all the positive forces inherent in mankind. It speaks about the future of Christened Man.

The Individual and his Destiny

Plato was possibly the first man to insist that we take full responsibility for our destiny instead of blaming bad luck, chance, the gods, the stars or God. Steiner too makes us realise that we are the makers of our destiny, that we live 'rightly' only if we totally accept our psychological personality with all its quirks and idiosyncracies as well as identify with our destiny, the opportunities which are given us and the adverse blows which meet us from 'outside'. This is not always easy. But as the existentialists have found, it is the only alternative to utter despair available to modern alienated man. Albert Camus shows this dilemma very clearly. *The Outsider* describes the despair of modern man who lives within a meaningless, joyless world; the doctor in *The Plague* depicts the same man triumphant. He is the man who without belief in God, without the dictates of tradition, custom, government or church takes fullest responsibility in a given situation which is not of his own making and which appears to be without hope. He identifies with his own moral understanding, and acts.

Contemporary Morality

Today, we are facing evil in quite novel ways. The cultures of the past built up strong traditions which moulded the young and continued to guide people throughout their lives. These traditions have largely broken down. Today, we can no longer say with certainty what is 'normal' and what is 'deviant'. Nor is there any institution with the natural authority to instil one universal form of behaviour into all of us. But all the time we are being tempted and persuaded by more powerful forces than those faced by peoples of earlier cultures. Whole industries are built on the exploitation of the young and on making them dependent on this or that product. Needs are elaborately created, a certain life style held up as a model, and all the refinements of psychology allied to the persuasive power of the media. Government and big business are the main benefactors because they have the greatest financial resources at their disposal for swaying us.

At the same time we are told by influential scientists that there is nothing to be explained. To look for meaning is 'pre-scientific', the aim of science is to manipulate the world and other beings to our greater advantage. Questions of right and wrong are no longer asked. The obvious result is that ever more people are simply out to increase their means of self-gratification. The new nihilism has become respectable and to such people the concerned man is an oddity. This again tends to help government, industry and business to control us ever more tightly as questions of principle are so rarely asked. Steiner would have been confirmed in his view that Lucifer and Ahriman, the two adversaries, always play into each other's hands.

When confronted with such problems the instinctive reply of many people of good will is to call for the restoration of 'standards', a return to traditional values. But also other people would like to go back to yesterday's attitudes. Usually they are frightened people, people worried about their social privileges, people unsure of their own ability to lead moral lives without firm outer constraints, or people frightened by an uncertain future at a time of rapid social change. They are the people who call for 'law and order'. But if they first looked at history they would realise that they are calling in vain. History is a one-way street. Innocence lost can never be regained.

Russians have never known political freedom. Officialdom strives to uphold old-fashioned moral standards. Children in school are seen, not heard. Love of the fatherland is still a matter of course. Pornography is illegal. The films on television would not have shocked our Victorian ancestors. The perverters of youth all seem to live in the West. The feeling of *moral* superiority is used to prove the *political* superiority of their system. But even with the full power of a repressive police state they have not succeeded. When we read how at the age of 16 Vladimir Bukovsky, the impeccable young communist, in one flash saw through the obscenity of a conformist system we rejoice: he had not adopted our sense of values of which at that time he knew nothing, but he had established his own morality, the only *true* morality, and thereby stood out against the society which had tried to press him into its own mould. When after Franco's death the heavy hand of a brutally enforced conformity was gradually and skilfully lifted from the Spanish people it soon became clear that the fascists' effort to turn the clock back had totally failed.

Rudolf Steiner would not even have tried. He saw in modern Western man the hope for the future. True, we are no happy spectacle, alienated, confused, uncertain as we are, but only he who has gone through the eye of the needle of the consciousness soul can hope to move into a better future. Steiner seems in this respect not so very different from Plato. He too had to confront the Ahrimanic manipulator in the person of Callicles in the *Gorgias*, while the brilliant, likeable immoralist Alcibiades appeared as a beguiling Lucifer. He did not find it difficult to show that *rationally* the position of neither the brutal fascist nor of the libertine was tenable. Beyond this he could only offer the example of his teacher Socrates and his imaginative stories, the inherent truth of which a sensitive listener might well perceive.

Over 2000 years later Steiner could be much more concrete and therefore much more helpful. While it is likely that Plato, and Aristotle as well, gave spiritual advice which was never written down, the bulk of Steiner's work is published so that anybody today can go to the nearest bookshop and buy what he thinks he needs. Out of the wealth of material we want here to look at three areas of advice only. The first area basing itself on the *Philosophy of Freedom* concerns individual morality. Like the existentialists, Steiner advises me to accept but not to identify with my psychological personality, but with my morality, the result of my unique karmic situation. This means the end of judgements. It also means the end of looking over one's shoulders and asking oneself what society, the church, even God expects one to do in a particular and unique situation. The choice is mine. In certain circumstances it can be a free choice. But I shall have to face the consequences. I make my choices, but my choices make and form me.

A second area which can be approached by meditation and contemplation is the awareness of the cosmic roots of my being. The exercises towards this awareness are many and varied. Once this experience is firmly established the meditant will appreciate the serenity of the early Christians who – among others – gave a vivid testimony to the primacy of the spiritual part of our being. The third area is that of Christ. We take the fallibility of man simply as a fact which warrants no undue comment, but we endeavour patiently to work towards a transformation which can but be gradual and is bound to meet with repeated failures and disappointments. But as experience shows, substantial progress can nevertheless be made, in our own development, in social relationships, in our dealings with the earth.

What Rudolf Steiner says, at least to the present author is: there is no way back to the relative security of bygone times. But we can build a true and modern form of moral life once we become aware of ourselves as beings of body, soul and spirit connected to the cosmos. A pious dream? No. We don't expect the world to change overnight, but just as the tiny minority of the Society of Friends have been able to work for gradual change, so people inspired by Steiner can have a try. Experience has shown that for the inner and outer work of anthroposophists no supermen are necessary, but that ordinary men and women can see the joys inherent in such an undertaking as the one described: to establish their own morality, to find their roots in the spirit and to learn a modern way to activate the Christian impulse of freedom and love.

Apocalyptic Horror

Worse than the fears which assail frightened people is the horror experienced by committed women and men. They have not forgotten the holocaust in which millions of Jews, gypsies and sexual deviants were murdered in obedience to a crooked ideology. To evaluate the enormity of this crime we must not forget that the organisers of the 'final solution' were members of one of Europe's most cultured people and that the victims had not committed any crime nor were they in any way a danger to the government of their day. Officially sanctioned murder and torture did not stop with the downfall of Hitler's *Reich*, but is the rule rather than the exception all over the world used against their opponents by whatever regime happens to be in power. Such things do not only occur in far-off countries, but also in Britain – for example in Ulster.

The horror of concerned people is increased when they realise that the perpetrators of torture, murder and rape are not necessarily perverts and villains, but ordinary women and men who otherwise seem to live very ordinary lives. Not so long ago the Greeks made a film which portrayed how at the time of the colonels' regime ordinary young men were systematically brutalised and turned into cruel torturers. One of them later reflected on what he had done and saw to it that his experiences and reflections were made the subject of this film. It seemed almost unimaginable what he had gone through since he had begun to face his actions. There he was seen in the film. His voice had become gentle, his face could remind one of Christ, and sheer horror befell the viewer: "Such is man, this is myself".

Some people might cynically turn their eyes away from this horror, but others can understand how man unprotected by the strong restraints of the past can easily fall prey to the two adversaries, more easily than ever before. We are, in St Paul's words, fighting against powers and principalities, and experience how frail and exposed modern man really is. But again and again the living Christ is experienced standing between the two adversaries revealing to us the enormous compass of our potential experience and the centre from which transformation and healing can spring.

Can it really? There can be no general answer in the abstract because when approaching Christ we step into a sphere of freedom, a sphere where the relation of cause and effect is not so obvious, a sphere where risks have to be taken. But on a more personal basis an answer can be given. The present author can look back at more than forty years' experience in teaching adolescents, some of them rather damaged and insecure. But also from the work of others with drug addicts, with young people without any hope, with criminals it is clear that transformation can work. *Can*, not *will*. We step out into a world of utter uncertainty, we do so without illusions, but with courage and confidence. We cannot reach our brothers in danger while we are firmly cushioned by a society which they disdained and left. We shall have to share their disdain and let them share in our humanity. What can start the process of transformation is their awareness of our autonomous morality and the buoyancy of lives lived beyond the confines of orthodox judgements and attitudes.

Death, Spiritual Existence, New Life on Earth

Let us after this interlude go back to Camus and his experience of the position of modern man, his tragedy in *The Outsider*, his triumph in *The Plague*. Steiner is able to put this attitude into a wider, cosmic context. As a man gets older an ever widening gap appears between his life's intentions and his actual achievement. After death, according to Steiner, man is able to work back through the experiences of his past life, to sift the essential from the superficial, to realise where he went wrong. Some of his wishes will disappear, others will turn into firm resolutions. As the time approaches when he gradually disassociates himself from a purely spiritual existence and looks towards his next earth life he becomes concerned with building up the right vehicle to realise his resolutions. A body has to be found to give him scope and a personality to be built up to allow him to live according to his needs and expectations. – It is, of course, obvious that it is never possible to realise all one's intentions as each one of us is connected with so many others who also have their needs and expectations. – But as a man enters bodily existence his powers grow weaker and greater beings working through his unconscious, the will in Steiner's terminology, and that of people close to him are active to bring about what he himself in his spiritual existence had planned. Innumerable incidents happen beyond our control, and yet they fit into a pattern, they eventually make sense. The personality of a man and what meets him from 'outside' are but the two sides of the same coin. This is what Steiner means by karma: the destiny which I planned for myself and which can be brought about partly by myself in my pre-natal state and partly by higher spiritual powers. This karma – to be precise, this *old karma*, as Steiner calls it – is ultimately I, at least as much, indeed more so than the shape of my face and the tone of my voice. So I learn to identify with it.

What Eastern thinking accepts as fate, as Allah's will, as the iron law of karma, to which man has to bow, is experienced by the Western and Christian teacher as I myself on the way towards self realisation, a process imbued with grace. Am I not allowed to help and to comfort where in a previous earth existence I had hurt and harmed? May I not feel that a situation which has got hopelessly wrong and with the best will in the world cannot be righted will be manageable in altered conditions after each one of the participants has been able to review the intricate network of relationships which brought about this intractable situation and has been able to do so with the help of superhuman insight, understanding and compassion? Thus the old karma is something which I and those around me have woven and which in this earth-life guides and sustains me and presents me with the tasks which I prescribed for myself on my path of development.

The New Karma

My past provides me with the raw material of my life: a particular body in a particular family, social setting, country and language, a particular psychological personality, a series of obstacles and opportunities. But they are only the raw material. What I do with all this is my very own affair and depends on my insight, courage, imagination and on my social intentions. Here on earth I act out of my own resources and, again, take full responsibility for what I am doing. I do not passively accept my destiny nor do I harken all the time to what arises out of my subconscious and persuade myself that premonitions, dreams, intimations and coincidences are identical with divine guidance. My responsibility is fully accepted as I realise that in shaping my life, in creatively 'playing' with the raw material of my existence I build *new karma*, the consequences of which will be with me for periods greater than the remainder of this earth-life. To face the fact that I am creating new karma needs courage, confidence and a strictly objective approach. It needs courage because I feel I am taking full responsibility for my future as well as for my past, it needs confidence in the presence of spiritual beings working in my destiny and presenting me with the possibility of continuing development, and it needs an objective attitude towards myself, my responsibilities and my motivation. But I may also feel that in this way I truly discharge the responsibilities of a free man.

The Integrity of Biography

One of the first consequences of positively responding to this widened perception of karma is a new attitude to one's biography, and that of one's fellow men. We become more objective towards our unfolding biography and fairly early in life can sense the boundaries within which this life is likely to unfold. We learn to take decisions which are in harmony with the objective demands which 'outer' circumstances make on us and we marvel at, and learn from the mysterious, but purposeful ways in which my life and that of others are intertwined. We follow the lives of our contemporaries in a way reminiscent of our listening to a symphony. As the music unfolds the clearer the intricacies of the composition become. We learn to look at others in a non-judgemental, compassionate way. Non-judgemental, because we realise that without knowledge of another person's karmic circumstances any judgement can at best be superficial and at worst totally destructive. Compassionate, because we realise that our friend and neighbour is exposed to the same onslaughts of Luciferic and Ahrimanic forces as we ourselves, that we all share the human predicament to have fallen out of the womb of nature and entered on the path towards freedom, a dangerous path on which there is no turning back and where progress is not easy to achieve.

The Existentialist Dilemma

We learn to take our individual responsibility seriously and we appreciate the absolutely different, indeed unique nature of the other's karma. But as Christians we are concerned not only with our own advance, but with the destiny of mankind in its totality. Our behaviour to our fellow men is our relationship to Christ Himself. This surely is the meaning of the word about "the least of my brethren". To resolve this dilemma means to learn the art of creating a space of freedom around us. We are encouraged to cast our bread upon the water, but whether fish or fowl will snap it up or whether it is simply dissolved by the water or rots on the shore is beyond the sphere of *our* discretion. This is a space where higher powers are able to act.

The Lord of Karma

So we learn to live within the balance of polarities, concerned with our fellow men, but not interfering, consciously responsible for our lives and yet aware of the guidance of higher powers, deeply aware of the strength, sometimes indeed the tragedy of karma. This, however, does not mean that we withdraw our compassion and look at the other's destiny 'objectively', that is, with an unfeeling heart. So we school ourselves to face after our death the Lord of Karma, Christ. He Who experienced the totality of human tragedy will understand our fallibility, our exposure to Lucifer and Ahriman. Through His guidance we learn to evaluate our past life, with the help of His wisdom and compassion we form our resolves for our future development.

Turning from the individual to mankind we see in the age-long conflicts and upheavals, in human attainment and human tragedy the slow and painful development of man destined for freedom, man gradually moving from being part of God's creative work to the state of a co-worker in the creative process. We are, in Steiner's words, on the way to becoming the tenth hierarchy.

PART III
The Path

Chapter Six
The Path

The way of inner schooling which Steiner opened up to his disciples is vastly different from many other ways of striving towards increased awareness. We shall therefore begin by saying what it is *not*. But even before doing so one other consideration will concern us. We can study Steiner's works, we can join the Anthroposophical Society without wishing to enter on this Path. We can confine ourselves to the study of Steiner's books and lectures, and find there such a wealth of material for our inner effort that we may not feel the need to enter into any other discipline as well. Indeed that is what many people are actually doing. They notice that the very act of reading Steiner's basic books, as e.g. *The Philosophy of Freedom* or *Theosophy* is in itself a kind of schooling which brings about a disciplined training of concentration, of thinking and imagination, and induces a need for contemplation and a certain amount of self observation, all essential ingredients of the Path. Why should we wish to go further? We are not bidden by Steiner to do so nor are there any outer rewards for him who decides to go this way.

What the Path is Not

First of all, we are not promised any spectacular results or sudden insights as certain hallucinogenic drugs and other practices can bring about, nor will it induce abrupt personality changes or relaxation and euphoria. Insights will come, a more balanced personality will arise, but this will be the fruit of the work of many months or years, perhaps of a lifetime. Development will be organic and healthy, gradual and steadying. It will not estrange the meditant from outer life, it will not necessitate any break with the ordinary activities in his family and in his work, indeed it may easily have the reverse effect of integrating him more strongly within his community and make him a fitter person in the sphere which he has chosen for his outer work.

Secondly, there is no guru. Rudolf Steiner never compelled or subjugated. He was a liberator of men. He, as it were, gave us a map of the terrain which we can traverse. The actual route which we follow will depend on our own needs and possibilities and on the conversations with our fellow wanderers. Never will we take a step in the dark or go by the bidding of some authority. As we proceed we are aware of what lies in front of us, we are free to explore that region which seems most promising to us, we can, if need be, retrace our steps.

Thirdly, we are not to expect an enhancement of our power over our fellow men nor insights into hidden depths which are the proud possession of some occult elite. We shall not know more than other, non-meditating anthroposophists, we shall at best know the same things in a different, more authentic and personal way. People in search of power or 'secret knowledge' will find that Steiner's advice is useless to them.

Handwritten margin notes: "V Negative", "How does he know", "Why? may it seems obvious that the writer knows not a lot and is a bit too self-opinionated for some one who is supposed to follow Steiners ideas,"

Towards Supersensible Knowledge

We shall find ourselves on a path towards supersensible knowledge, but this path begins not by throwing away sense-derived experiences, but, on the contrary, by sharpening these experiences. To take for example an ordinary conversation. We probably start by listening to the meaning of the words, possibly by not even listening exactly because we disagree with something our partner has just said and so we wait for the moment when we can have our say, meanwhile perhaps rehearsing our counter-arguments. But as we train ourselves we learn to listen to the whole of his speech and try actively to think the other's thoughts. We learn to listen to the tone of his voice, the rhythm of his speaking, the flow of his phrases. We observe the gestures of his hands, the movement of his eyes, the way he uses his body. We do not analyse or rationalise these impressions, but use them as a means by which our partner is able to speak to us about himself. In the end we shall be unable to say what was communicated via the eye, what via the ear, what was an intimation, what came across beyond the field of *sense* impressions. We were able to establish an existential communication where being spoke to being, where we became a receptive organ which our partner could make use of. Only after the experience is over and our partner gone shall we be able to articulate what happened in this meeting of being with being.

Two points can be made now about the experience described. Where is the border between sense experience and supersensible experience? It is undefined and fluid and lies, of course, within ourselves. We can learn to shift this boundary and to cross it. People who have succeeded will notice to their intense surprise how much stronger and more direct supersensible experiences are than sense experiences. They realise that our senses act like filters which dim down the dynamic fullness and the intensity of supersensible experience.

Communion

We have learned to commune with other people. So we may go on and equally learn to commune with plants and animals, with angels and other spiritual entities, and with the dead. This latter exercise may be particularly rewarding, provided we act not out of curiosity or other selfish reasons, but out of an honest wish to continue our loving relationship to those who have left the sense world, and to help them.

Clarity: Thinking

It may have been noticed already that Steiner's way is one of increasing clarity. Thinking and close observation are our starting points, a pre-occupation with semi-conscious phenomena is considered most unhelpful. Dreams, premonitions, coincidences, 'vibrations' lie outside our scope. These realms are shot through with our unconscious wishes and passions and so we cannot rely on the validity of what they seem to tell us. Such messages might have had a place in earlier pre-scientific cultures, today they hinder and disturb the progress of modern man. Steiner did his utmost to discourage people who relied on atavistic forms of clairvoyance. They had to unlearn what came from past modes of experience before they entered on the Path. The trained scientist, on the other hand was welcome. Indeed, Steiner helped him further to develop his powers of thinking and observation as for instance in his valuable booklet *Practical Training in Thought*[1] which constitutes a firm basis for those who wish to gain reliable insights.

Sanity: Health of Mind and Body

Next to clarity comes sanity. The point of the exercises is gradually to increase the range and intensity of our experiences. Therefore care must be taken that people who are being overwhelmed by their ordinary every-day experiences do not enter on the Path. Intensified experiences could have a shattering effect on them. Equally people whose bodily health is frail may find the exercises too strenuous for them. On the other hand, those who are simply in need of increased mental health can only be helped by the discipline of the *preparatory* exercises, such as those in the booklet mentioned above or the Six Exercises in *Knowledge of the Higher Worlds*. Many people who work with Steiner's exercises feel that they result not only in an improvement in mental health – among the more immediate goals are control of emotions and thoughts, presence of mind, courage, equanimity , etc. – but that also their bodily health improves through the gradual integration of their personality and their increased ability to face stresses and strains.

If we observe how our mind usually works we shall discover two main activities. Both happen automatically like independent mechanisms. A sense impression arouses a certain mental image in us which leads by association to a series of loosely connected memories, pictures or concepts. I hear the sound of a trumpet and a memory arises of a brass band which I heard in my youth. My father stood beside me and I muse on this man who was so close to me and yet so aloof. How do I behave towards my daughters? Have I been more open to them? So it goes on within me, uncontrolled and without a goal, triggered off by the sound of a trumpet.

The other activity occurs when I observe attentively and react to ever-changing sense data in as positive a manner as possible. This happens for instance when I drive a car. These two modes of mental behaviour, the one totally automatic, the other largely reactive may sometimes seem to be our only ways of mental activity. But everybody who has been able to be engaged in a concentrated thought activity knows otherwise. There are various and quite different stages of consciousness. The aim of the Path is to discover some new forms of consciousness where everything happens as I will it. In doing so we acquire a new identity. We become aware of deeper layers of our being, more spiritual and – astonishingly – more real than our experiences up to now. We are on the way to discover our Self.

Some Hindrances

A break-through to those deeper levels of being is not easily achieved. Over many centuries we Europeans have become increasingly interested in the sense world, sometimes to the exclusion of any other interest. Our contemporary Western civilisation increases this development enormously. It assails us by an almost continuous flood of sense impressions, visual and acoustic, and by a never-ending flow of new information which we have time neither to appreciate fully nor to assimilate. Our education tends to direct us to superficial yes-no answers. We suffer from stresses which were unknown even one or two generations ago. When we seek relaxation we too often sit in front of a screen and even our holidays are sometimes spent *en masse* and surrounded by noise. To learn to be alone and silent is now a major achievement for us.

Discovering the Inner Life

Yet it is not impossible to imagine what a change of consciousness means and what it is to discover an inner realm. Suppose we are sitting in a concert hall. We notice how the hall fills with people, the orchestra assembles, finally the conductor arrives. The music begins. We watch the conductor's antics, but soon we get bored. We count how many ladies wear red. Then the miracle happens. Ladies, conductor, players, the concert hall itself have disappeared and an entirely different world has opened up. Our total environment is the music of Stravinsky.

The entry into this world of music is not automatic. We have to be unusually gifted or have to have a special training. Even then, we cannot always be sure that we can shake off the every-day world sufficiently to enter into this newly-discovered realm. But to leave this realm is easier. There may be a period afterwards in which it may be difficult to return to normal conversation. For a few days some musical themes may continue to haunt us. In course of time – if we continue our efforts – we shall feel very much at home in this realm of music, a realm of inner experience with but tenuous links to what we might call the world of utility. Nevertheless, we may easily feel that these musical experiences are more important to us than most other events, and that they are making us richer, better and more profound.

There are many similarities between the way we learn to appreciate music and the opening up of the Path. There *exists* a field of inner experience from which the unmusical is excluded. But through consistent practice, concentration and study also the less gifted person can penetrate this world to a certain extent, far enough to appreciate the unique quality of musical experience, even if he never develops a spontaneous enjoyment of Webern. The effort necessary for success on the Path is considerably greater. Not only is it necessary to create an inner space free of the play of associations, memories, sense impressions, passions and fixed concepts, but every bit of the inner experience has to be created by ourselves, it is not given to us by a great composer. We have to develop to the full our powers of concentration, imagination and contemplation.

The Question of Autosuggestion

The critical reader will rightly object here: "If the inner experience has to be wholly created by ourselves how can it possibly be objective?" This question does, indeed, demand a careful answer. If two people witness the same event and recollect their impressions to each other they will often find that, apparently, they were sensitive to entirely different features. What they experienced related to their expectations, to different previous experiences, to their mood and temperament, and to their education which enabled the one to conceptualise and articulate certain parts of the experience which the other completely overlooked. We may almost say: we only experience what we are prepared for and expect. A boy of fifteen years once said to his teacher after they had studied basic geomorphology that the daily bus journey to and from school had quite suddenly completely changed from a dreary routine to an exciting adventure. What had been meaningless before now spoke to him strong and clear. The 'objective' facts had always been present, but now for the first time the mind was directed towards them and had learned to appreciate and conceptualise them. It is probable that many people have spiritual experiences which, however, they are unable to recognise for what they are. These experiences are, particularly at first, fleeting and insubstantial. In addition, the untrained person will be devoid of concepts to enable him to articulate to himself what has happened to him and thereby give the experience some permanence. Although there are exceptions we can formulate the principle: Only when the possibility of conceptualising an experience exists can it be raised into consciousness. So *one* of the preconditions for spiritual development is a certain amount of information of what might happen on the Path.

This is, however, not the full answer to the objection of autosuggestion. It is in truth not easy to distinguish between creations of one's subconscious and genuine spiritual experiences. In normal consciousness we have access to objective and concrete data which allow us to evaluate and check our experiences. Such data are lacking in supersensible experiences. We have therefore to train ourselves to an ever-increasing searching and critical attitude towards ourselves, our motivations, our prejudices, the idiosyncracies of our particular personality, and rigorously discard as useless all experiences which raise the slightest doubt. If we proceed with proper discrimination and never allow ourselves to be taken in by vanity or haste we shall come across new experiences which are not only totally unexpected and unconditioned by what we ourselves are, but which also manifest an entirely new dimension, the experience of which so far has been beyond our ken.

Preparatory Exercises

We can better appreciate now why Steiner emphasises so strongly the value of preliminary exercises. They teach us three different qualities. We have to learn concentration and imagination as the basis for future meditative work, we have to learn to question our motivations in order to shed as many illusions about ourselves as possible, and we have to progress in the field of morality. While the critical attitude to ourselves combined with an increasing ability to concentrate and to experience sensitively leads to an enrichment and remodelling of our personality, moral progress brings about enhanced responsibility. Like the great Buddha's, Steiner's way is useless to him who is not willing to practise an enhanced morality. Steiner states that for every step in spiritual progress three steps have first to be taken in the field of morality. This, obviously, is to ensure that what spiritual truths may later be experienced will be used with greatest responsibility and never for selfish ends. Among Steiner's pupils there was a civil engineer who had such gifts as a healer that he was able to give up his profession and simply practise healing. This man asked Steiner whether he would teach him new skills beyond those which were part of his natural endowment. Steiner obliged, but put him under obligation never to make money whenever he used any of the techniques which he had learned from him.

Among the preparatory exercises we want to mention specifically two activities: a loving concern for nature and the contemplation of human destiny. Both these activities are comparatively easy, but can result in an unexpected inner bounty. To study the colours and forms of semi-precious stones, to care for a few plants, to observe the behaviour of birds and other animals in their natural habitat, to know the stars in the sky and follow their movements, to learn to 'read' the shape and movement of the clouds and to forecast the weather: these are studies which Steiner advised us to take up. We are learning to read in the book of nature, so rich and wonderful. We are acquiring an understanding of *processes*, an awareness of the constant flux of things, and yet we uncover meaning in all these ever-changing manifestations. We learn to appreciate the blossoms of spring as much as the ripe fruits and falling leaves of autumn. Growth and decay, birth and death, youth and old age are part of the same process which unites man with all the kingdoms of nature and with the cosmos within which our planet functions. We learn to observe more closely, to appreciate beauty, to interrelate function and form, to understand the wisdom-filled processes which each fleeting phenomenon points to, we learn to connect and stand in amazement and awe before the wonderful creation within which we have our existence.

Possibly even more important is the study of human life, of our own biography and that of others. Again we stand in awe before the events of birth and death, before the tragedies which can engulf a human life as well as before the enormous gifts which are incessantly being showered upon us. Here too we become sensitive to structure and meaning and learn an equanimity towards what befalls us and ever greater compassion for our neighbour.

Meditation

The time may have come to state in simple terms what Rudolf Steiner's form of meditation is. We have already indicated some of the pre-conditions and preparatory exercises, and we also stated what this form of meditation is not. The aim is best described by reference to Steiner's description of the development of mankind. While earlier forms of meditation often strove after a withdrawal of all Ego activity so that the creative powers of the universe could fully play into and enlighten man, Steiner, the modern teacher, attempts to *raise* the consciousness of the meditant to such heights that he learns to communicate with spiritual and divine beings.

Meditation takes place – here most teachers will agree – in the inner space which a man prepares. Into this space of silence, peace and absence of sensations originating in the world of the senses the meditant places a series of mental images. He uses his powers of concentrated thinking not in order to think as he is wont to do, but to keep open the space which he himself has created and array a progression of images, sounds, words or mental pictures in a way which he had determined before the beginning of the exercise. At certain moments he will empty his consciousness completely, – without, however, falling into dreaming or into sleep. He will progress slowly, trying to experience to the fullest degree the images or words which he puts in strict sequence into the inner space which he himself has created. As he attempts to achieve full concentration and to prepare a field for his creative, but strictly disciplined picture-forming imagination he will also strive to be fully involved on the emotional plane, the realm of feeling, with the pictures he himself is creating. The exercise will be consciously concluded and then a period of contemplation, or musing may follow. In this latter activity the experience is further integrated, the tender young shoot of the meditative experience wedded to memories of the past and insights of the present. Conscious and subconscious elements flow together and without pressing for articulation a certain evaluation of the experience may now take place. The whole exercise does not take over-long. Steiner suggests five to ten minutes for the beginner. While the exercise demands such inner strength as the meditant is able to muster, the conclusion, when successful, brings a feeling of new strength, an awareness of bodily and mental well-being.

Verses and Meditations

The exercises which Steiner describes most frequently and which we therefore need only mention here, the rose cross and the seed of grain,[2] are concerned with the production of mental images. But at many occasions he also used poetic formulations either to summarise the content of a lecture or to sustain one or more people in a particular situation or task. A number of these texts are available in English and I would particularly recommend George and Mary Adams' translations in *Verses and Meditations* which contain also the German originals, and Owen Barfield's *The Participated Year*.[4] These verses cover a large part of Steiner's work and extend roughly over the last twenty years of his life. They range in character from pure poetic utterances to *mantras*, the Indian word for sacred texts which through their very texture –

quality of sound, metre, rhythm, stress, grammatical structure, etc. – convey profound intimations of spiritual reality.

While the non-verbal exercises – the two main ones were quoted above – open up most easily for people with a strong visual memory, the verses provide a good starting point for those who are particularly sensitive to musical and poetic values. He who lives for some time with one or more of these verses will notice how they appeal to his conscious being as much as to his subconscious and how they help to integrate the two. Our first question will be: what does this verse mean? For, as always with Steiner, there is no room for the instinctive rumblings of our subconscious unchecked. But as we proceed to enter into the texture of the verse, as we learn to 'play' creatively with its various artistic elements, less conscious parts of our being are stirred, and their activity in turn increases our verbal and conceptual understanding. What began almost as a logical exercise – "What do these words actually mean?" – gradually, possibly over years, becomes a profound experience. The texts which have become familiar to us turn into an invaluable treasure which can accompany us through life and shed light on and provide help in many a trial.

Decision Making

We shall mention a last example, a very practical one, to show how we learn to integrate our conscious life with the unconscious and how – if we proceed with care and caution – greater powers may be able to help us. Suppose we are faced with a clear yes-no decision. We shall neither try to think this out on logical grounds alone – real life is beyond logics – but neither shall we abdicate our responsibility and leave the decision to a spontaneous whim. Nor shall we persuade ourselves that, provided we have no will of our own either way, we shall hear the voice of God speaking to us and solve our dilemma for us. More likely, we should hear the voice of our subconscious and have the satisfaction of being able to do what we really wanted to do all along, as well as having the exalted feeling of having left the decision to a higher power.

Steiner's advice is different. We rely fully on our conscious power of judgement and take complete responsibility for our action, but proceed so that help *may* be given to us. In the evening before falling asleep we visualise as concretely as possible what the consequences of our action would be. But we refrain from judgement. We then imagine with equal concentration what the consequences would be if we were *not* to take this course of action. We then remove the whole question out of our mind and fall asleep. We do this on the next two evenings as well, but if the matter is very urgent one evening will have to do. On the next morning we do the exercise for a last time. Again we visualise to the very best of our ability, first, all the likely consequences of our action and then those of our not acting. Whereas three days ago we felt there was little or nothing to choose between the two possibilities we now will feel, with surprise and gratitude, that only the one can in truth be considered. We have used our ordinary human faculties, we used them responsibly and to the full, but by withholding judgement the powers which help us to live out of our rightful karma have had the possibility to join in the decision for which we now take full responsibility.

Growing Roots

We have learned to clear an inner space free of automatic and involuntary processes of our physical organisation and our subconscious. We have learned to stand back and withhold judgement. The result can be that *super-conscious* higher beings can use this space and enliven our thoughts and will. The result of these endeavours will be that by and by we grow roots in the spirit. We acquire a new identity, the identity of a spiritual entity, of a cosmic being. To put it into an older form of language: we acquire Faith in the meaning in which St Paul used the word. He did not mean 'belief', he himself never believed, but doubted until there came his experience before Damascus. Faith meant to him standing firm and never losing hold of what he had spiritually experienced, to witness in any situation to the primacy of spiritual reality. Such faith does change us. Things will take on an entirely new character, the world will appear a dense network of relationships which embrace the living, the dead, the divine hierarchies and also the kingdoms of nature. We shall not only have gained an increase in understanding, but also acquired more inner strength and peace, and refined our emotions.

In retrospect, a few points shall be re-affirmed. Our progress has been slow, but steady and gradual. Probably we went through periods when we doubted the efficacy of our exercises, possibly there were times when we felt negligent. But if we dealt responsibly with our exercises, if after every failure and disappointment we quietly got up and went on, if most of all, we remained persistent in our effort and did not lose sight of our goal we shall in the end feel that our efforts were not wasted and that, imperceptibly, we grew and changed. We may feel joy at the fact that we belong to a community of meditants who do not strive for secret knowledge, for power or psychological bliss, but who look at their daily effort as a service to mankind, to the earth and to the universe.

Readers who want to study these matters further might wish to read George Adams' preface to *Verses and Meditations* or Paul Eugen Schiller's *Rudolf Steiner and Initiation*.[5] The latter offers a clear and systematic survey of the Path written in Steiner's terms, the former gives wise guidance about the practice of meditation and some related subjects. The most important works by Steiner in print today which deal with the Path are to be found in the bibliography.

PART IV
Social and Cultural Initiatives

Chapter Seven
Building Alternatives

The Anthroposophical Movement has two closely connected aspects. One is contemplative and meditative, the other outgoing, dynamic, practical. Although in his own life each anthroposophist will have to resolve the tension between these two attitudes there is no inherent conflict between them. This polarity arises directly from the situation in which we find ourselves today and which Steiner anticipated early this century. He experienced early mankind embedded in the collective life of the tribe, in the rhythms of nature and of the universe, but very gradually we detached ourselves from these gentle constraints. In more recent history we broke with the traditions of family, nation and church. So we became individualised and experienced the misery and glory of autonomous man. We became estranged from each other and alienated from the world, but for the first time we are able to lead our lives according to our *own* insights. In this process of individuation we destroyed a substantial part of our environment and fragmented society. Most people sensitive to this situation have a yearning to go back to our origins. Not so Steiner. To him the process of individuation is neither a gigantic mistake nor a misfortune, but a necessary step in the maturation of man, who now has to shoulder immense responsibilities.

These responsibilities might seem unbearable for us unless we learn to focus on the pivotal point in the history of this planet, the Mystery of Golgotha. Through it the selfhood of man became sanctified and the possibility of transformation, of renewal established. The Christian task is one of healing and the ideal conditions for it come about where two or three – or more – form a new community, one not built on tradition or natural affinity, but on the free resolve of the participants. Through meditation, prayer and contemplation we become aware of our spiritual dimension. Gradually real insights are gained and new strengths won, and these can then be utilised in our tremendous tasks.

The God-given order of nature and of society lies in ruins. The new world can only be based on man. But man does, of course, not only consist of a body, he has a spiritual dimension as well as inalienable needs of his soul. A society based on the needs of the body alone must be rapacious, destructive, inhuman. Many an anthroposophist sees his task in building a new world, a world based on the full acceptance of the humanity of man.

Anthroposophy has therefore not only a contemplative side, but is also a dynamic movement for social, artistic and scientific renewal which has produced schools and workshops, curative homes and banks, hospitals and schools, organisations for social development and farms, laboratories and trading organisations. All these institutions are independent of each other and work not for the benefit of some privileged anthroposophists, but for anybody who wishes to avail himself of the services offered. Anthroposophy displays the same basic features as the Society of Friends: the cultivation of an inner life, utter respect for the freedom of the individual, social action for the benefit of all.

Common Features

There are certain characteristics common to all these activities. Most are based on an interesting mixture – not easily achieved – of individual initiatives and common responsibility. Usually, we find a healthy absence of hierarchy. At a Steiner school, to take one example, there is no headmaster, no board of governors, no heads of department. Thus each teacher works within a wide area of discretion as far as his own teaching is concerned. Matters of policy are decided by the College of Teachers, a republic of teachers which discusses all relevant issues and appoints officers to carry out the decisions made.

In an anthroposophical hospital a team of doctors, nurses and therapists will sit down to discuss the problems and the progress of their patients. They do not look at a particular patient as the liver case in Ward 2B, but as a person who is to be helped to overcome an illness which may be of special significance in his biography. Help is given by means of medicaments, diet, baths, massage, counselling, artistic therapy, whatever might be appropriate. The patient is made to understand what is the matter with him and what part he himself can play towards his recovery. Or if he cannot be healed he is helped to approach death in a dignified and conscious manner.

This illustrates also a second point of general validity: in all anthroposophical activities man is taken seriously, as part of mankind with its important tasks, and as an individual with his own unique biography.

No Commands and No Utopia

From what has been said in previous chapters it follows that no anthroposophist is under any obligation to give part of his time, let alone his whole life to some form of service. If he chooses an 'anthroposophical' profession this is his way of self-realisation. He is not looked upon as a 'better' anthroposophist, a more moral being, one who sacrifices himself to the cause. Whether he works for the inland revenue, as a priest or in the armed services, whether he teaches for the local education authority or in a Steiner school is his concern alone.

Steiner did not prescribe any course of action, nor did he lay down a blueprint for reform. If people felt a need for action and came to him for advice he would never refuse to assist. But the advice he gave was given to individuals with their special gifts and limitations, and it was given for a special, unique situation. His advice amounts to possible models, it was never intended as a blueprint as he himself emphasised in his Oxford lectures.¹ If we wish to realise some of his intentions we might ask ourselves first of all what these intentions really were, and how they were shaped and narrowed down by the conditions of his day and the gifts and limitations of the first anthroposophical practitioners in a special field. Then we might proceed to discover what we ourselves may be able to do within our limitations and in the altered conditions of our age.

When working with teachers Steiner continuously stated that he hoped to bring about a new *art* of education, thereby emphasising the creative role which each teacher, the educational artist, could play. If people later spoke about a *method* and called it perhaps the Waldorf method they committed a twofold betrayal of Steiner. They divorced the work from the man who inspired it, and they began to establish a new tyranny: "This is the way things are done here."

A Challenge

Each worker in an anthroposophical institution faces a creative tension between the traditions of his working place and his own initiatives and impulses. If the traditions become dominant and are perhaps enforced by constant reference to Rudolf Steiner or the founder of the particular institution the individual co-worker is likely to feel enslaved and his freedom and creativity – central to anthroposophical work – are jeopardised. But equally destructive is the person who simply insists on his right to be himself and who utterly disregards what to his colleagues seems an inalienable feature of any work related to Rudolf Steiner. Membership of a group responsible for an anthroposophical institution is therefore a real challenge. Such membership offers immense opportunities for learning more about oneself, about the nature of one's work and about Steiner's intentions, and helps us to acquire new social skills. As each institution is self-governing there exists today a wide variety of social practices and a considerable experience of how free individuals can actively co-operate in their daily work and arrive at common decisions.

Development

Much of the practical work done today by anthroposophists arose only after Steiner's death. In the field of education his intentions had become fairly clear and he had many opportunities to deal with practical questions in the life of the *Waldorfschule* during the first five years of its existence. Other activities can rely only on a much smaller amount of specific help from him, while there are also areas where anthroposophists built up activities without any specific advice from Steiner, relying simply on their own understanding of what the anthroposophical impulse is about. Two such areas are the banking foundations and the institutes for organisational development.

But even in the school movement a good deal of development has taken place. A certain professionalism based on over sixty years of experience has been developed, the aims of Steiner education have been realised in a wide variety of social environments and national cultures, there has been a fair amount of research, new areas of action opened up and old attitudes questioned. It is a remarkable fact that in Jaerna, a Swedish village, we find two Steiner schools side by side, each with its own distinctive education policy.

The above remarks seem necessary before we now set out to look in more detail at some anthroposophical activities. As we can only point to some general features we must dispel the idea that there are unified systems in education, medicine, the arts, etc. To really understand what happens in anthroposophical institutions means to visit them, to experience the life pulsating in them and to converse with some of their practitioners.

The Arts

As mentioned earlier Steiner's first major venture into practical activities was the production of plays. From this developed a number of new impulses for various art forms. There seem to be at least two motivations for Steiner's involvement in the arts. Repeatedly he stressed the limitations of language for expressing supersensible experiences and so he used every opportunity to point to the underlying spiritual realities through other media than words which are, after all, shaped in, and for the use of, the sense world. But he also appreciated the great value of artistic activities for the inner development of his pupils. They were able to cultivate spontaneity, imagination and inner discipline in a way which later would benefit their meditative life.

The Anthroposophical Society is no society for the cultivation of the arts. Its aims are quite different. But it would be difficult, perhaps impossible, to find another society, say, the Pilgrims' Trust or the Friends of the Earth, whose members take art as seriously as do anthroposophists. Not only do a good proportion of anthroposophists enjoy works of art and feel deeply concerned about them, many also actively pursue artistic activities. The name 'workshop' did not originate among them, but they had such workshops long before the name became widely known. They engaged in artistic activities in which the finished work was of lesser importance than the creative process and its results for the participants.

The Cognitive Value of the Arts

The scientific method as such is not questioned by the anthroposophist. He will, however, ask how far a scientific statement is relevant and whether a scientific invention is life-supporting or otherwise. When man is described to us as a naked ape or as a machine we may ask what relevance such a description has for our existence and self awareness. Are the most important facts perhaps distorted in such definitions or even suppressed? Which other creature known to man, let alone which machine, is aware that it is going to die one day? Which other creature is aware of our need for love, of its joys, tensions and pitfalls? But there are few, if any facts more important to each of us than are *eros* and *thanatos*, to use Freudian language. Often the artist can tell us much more about ourselves and our world than can the scientist. He can speak about the totality of existence where the scientist can offer us but specialised data. He can probe the depths of the mystery of human nature where the scientist will come up with abstract theories. An anthroposophist who aims at an *understanding* through reliving a process and at communion with other creatures can learn greatly from the insights of the artist. He or she will be aware that many great artists of this century had similar aims, people like Paul Klee and Henry Moore, Kandinsky and Rilke, to name only a very few. This cognitive element in the experience of art, art as a groping forward into the mysteries of existence, unites the anthroposophists with the most progressive and radical artists of this century.

Art of this Century

Anthroposophical art belongs to this century. It does not attempt to harken back to earlier modes of expression, its statements are consonant with the consciousness of our age. Steiner himself was, if anything, in advance of his age. He sketched the first large-scale building in pre-stressed concrete. His paintings in the cupola of the first Goetheanum manifest a power and dynamism not seen before the time of Cubists and Expressionists. He also pointed towards functionalism. A boiler house or a transformer station boldly proclaimed their function, a staircase was to invite the visitor to ascend, a door made clear where the handle was to be found. Much of his purely artistic work tended towards non-representative art, the identifiable object giving way to movement of form and qualities of colour.

A Spiritual Dimension

Notwithstanding the contemporary nature of anthroposophical art there also appear a number of divergent features. It does not encourage the artist to 'express' himself, but to mediate between the world and the beholder. It never denies man's humanity and spirituality. It is life-affirming and does not *exclusively* emphasise the squalor, cruelty and aggression inherent in our times.

Often we find a spiritual, even hieratic dimension, – most strongly experienced, perhaps, in the Dornach speech chorus. Many anthroposophical artists have been able to give expression to a truly modern religious feeling. But there is also another way of overcoming materialistic values in art: humour. Firmly embedded in Steiner's artistic intentions, it finds expression in the great centre piece for the Goetheanum, the wooden statue of Christ, the representative of mankind. Christ is shown holding the balance between the two adversaries. This awe-inspiring drama is watched by an impish head, establishing humour as a cosmic principle. Humour is hardly ever absent from performances of eurythmy, an art form which is singularly able to span the whole gamut of emotions from the ridiculous and fanciful to the ethereal and sublime.

Respect for Material

The anthroposophical artist and craftsman often shows great respect for the material he is working with, and attempts to bring out its particular qualities. Substance, colour, texture as well as form, tone and lighting will combine to express nuances incapable of verbal articulation. Respect for the materials which nature provided often results in a contemplative mood which surrounds the work produced. We experience the wood, the glass, the pigment, they, having been taken seriously, can speak to us and are not overpowered by the creativity and wilfulness of the artist.

Social and Therapeutic

Of course, great artists are as rare in the Anthroposophical Society as anywhere else. But the shaping spirit is at work in this society. As soon as anthroposophists have an activity going, a school, a therapeutic village or a meeting house, they are anxious to give it shape. They are aware of the *one* world, the unity of the spiritual and material, and, unlike the Puritan, do not like an environment alien to the activity taking place within it. Their artistic sensitivities are turned to social ends. Typically, there exists in England a group of anthroposophists who work under the name of Colour for Buildings. They specialise in the sensitive use of colour for the indoor and outdoor walls of buildings of widely different functions. Painting, eurythmy, speech and sculpture have all branched out into therapeutic activities. In this development, which was entirely spontaneous and not directed from any centre, the Christian inspiration of Anthroposophy may be seen at work.

A Final Question

Is there a recognisable anthroposophic art? Should there be such a thing? Did Rudolf Steiner give suggestions which any artist, regardless of his opinions, might take up? The present writer thinks that once such questions are faced the answer will be found fairly easily out of the totality of Steiner's ideas. He showed us possibilities which creative people might freely take up. He encouraged individual creativity and responsibility. He constantly emphasised the importance of art for individual development and its relevance in social renewal. He explored for himself a great variety of new techniques. He showed ways in which man's spiritual nature and striving can be artistically expressed in modern terms. He taught us respect for material substances. These are impulses which can be taken up in a wide variety of ways and by people of widely differing outlook. It seems unlikely that he was aiming for narrowmindedness, sectarianism and reliance on one particular technique in the pursuit of art when the opposite approach is so significant in his work in the Anthroposophical Society.

Education

Probably the most successful activity, so far, which arose out of Steiner's lifework is the Steiner school movement. We mentioned already how Steiner helped in building up the *Waldorfschule* in Stuttgart and how widely these schools have since spread. There exists a considerable amount of literature on various aspects of these schools[2] and so we need not go into details here. Our concern is the connection of this unique form of education with the totality of Steiner's insights.

Anthroposophical Schools?

It must be stated quite unmistakably that the aim of Steiner schools is not the care of the children of anthroposophists. The *Waldorfschule* arose out of the impulse to give culturally deprived children an all-round education and not simply occupational training. Nor do these schools aim at 'converting' children and young people to anthroposophy. Most old scholars of Steiner schools would be hard put to it if they had to answer the question: what did Rudolf Steiner really teach? Pupils will, of course, realise that their school is an unconventional school. Some may admire their teachers for being unorthodox, others might be embarrassed by the lack of conformity. Some of the features which will naturally be experienced by the pupils are the very wide curriculum, the strong involvement of the teacher with both his work and his pupils, the creative and artistic methods employed and the absence of textbooks or audio-visual courses.

A Question of Perception

At the beginning of this century teachers often felt that their noblest task was to ensure continuity of tradition. They had to hand on the values of past ages to future generations. Some looked at their pupils as potential empire builders. So they tried to toughen them up, and give them a sense of discipline and fair play. What does the contemporary teacher see in his pupils? A generation who might halt Britain's industrial decline? Future Oxbridge material? The vanguard of the revolution?

Not so the anthroposophist. He will experience *each* of his pupils, even the least endowed, as a being of body, soul and spirit. The sulky girl in front of me, the naughty boy playing me up behind my back are spiritual entities who happened to have incarnated some years after me. They are of the same stuff as I, they are essentially my equals. Where such an attitude prevails a child will rarely be humiliated.

But at the same time the teacher will be sensitive to individual differences. He will not expect his pupils to be uniform. He is aware of the uniqueness of a man's karma and therefore of the immense differences in human endowment. These differences cannot be judged by others, – unless the karmic reasons for, say, this total lack of artistic gifts are perceived. The teacher will painstakingly search for individual characteristics. They will tell him what kind of person he is facing and so enable him to help the individual pupil reach his own full potential. If he succeeds, as many teachers do, each pupil will feel recognised, appreciated and strengthened.

The Best Teaching Aid, the Teacher

If these are our basic attitudes the role of the teacher becomes paramount. Education towards humanity, education for freedom is only possible when the main emphasis is laid on human relationships.

At a Steiner school the teacher feels responsible for establishing a relationship of trust to *each* of his pupils, for building up her class into a well-integrated social group and for being a mediator between the class and the world. At every stage one will endeavour to bring the full reality of the world – natural as well as social – to one's children, but to do so in a way which corresponds to their emotional and intellectual development. One relates them to the world and knows that an education bereft of human values leads to alienation and lack of purpose. So Steiner schools have developed the practice of handing over responsibility for a given class to *one* teacher who will, for eight years, be their companion and teach them most subjects.

In order to mediate properly between the given world and a group of children it is necessary to enter fully into each subject under consideration. No longer is it enough to find a suitable textbook and then issue work sheets to one's pupils to test how far the subject matter has been understood. In this way only a superficial contact with the subject matter in hand is established, and this only on the intellectual level. The Steiner school teacher will attempt to involve the class emotionally and practically with the study in hand and so arouse interest and active involvement. To this end many subjects are taken in block periods, extending over the first two hours each school day for three or four weeks. This would make it possible in a block period on China to cook, serve and eat a Chinese meal, to use Chinese brush strokes in writing or to paint a landscape the Chinese way. So the class gets a taste of a different way of life and form of experience, and is not fobbed off with abstract facts and statistics.

Phases

It will be obvious to any reader of this book that the attitudes described here are firmly rooted in the totality of Steiner's view of the world. Equally important is, however, another aspect of his teaching which so far we have not met. In the course of his life a man goes through different stages which present various opportunities for outer activity and inner development.[3] This is of particular importance in childhood and youth. So Steiner gave to teachers many far-reaching indications about the development of our bodies, souls and minds in the first twenty years of our development. After Steiner's death Jean Piaget, Professor of Psychology at Geneva, investigated, completely independently of Steiner, similar aspects of human development. His exact findings confirm Steiner's more intuitive, but also more broadly-based statements: In our development we go through qualitatively different stages, none of which can be missed out and the order of which cannot be reversed.

When translated into practice – and Steiner schools have done this for almost seventy years – this means another fundamental shift of emphasis. By and large, it is the careers aspect which dominates the syllabus of many of our schools. At the age of eighteen the pupil is to have so much knowledge and certain specific skills in order to qualify for entrance to university, the professions, commerce, industry. In order to reach this target he should at the age of fifteen know so and so much, and such and such amount at twelve, at nine, at six years. He is seen as an adult in miniature.

Steiner disagrees. The human being at seven, at fourteen or at any age has a natural and fully integrated experience of the world which we should not distort by one-sidedly fostering certain qualities and neglecting most other aspects of experience. Rather we should see that at any age the specific potential of this age is realised to the full. There is an optimum age for most things: for climbing trees and for appreciating poetry. So we shall try to imbue any of these stages with the fullest amount of activity and experience specific to this age. We might call this the principle of permanent maturity. Children will then experience the full compass of human existence and, as experience shows, will be well equipped to cope with the many and varied demands of adult life.

The behaviourist school of psychology has proved that it is possible to interfere with the development of children and make them do things prematurely, completely out of phase. This can be achieved by manipulative practices which have nothing in common with the biological and psychological development of man. They have proved that it *can* be done. They did not ask at what price it can be done. The price to be paid is increased alienation, an inability to relate at any deeper level to others in the peer group, and a general impoverishment of the emotions. This is, of course, of little concern to people who believe in the manipulative practices of Huxley's *Brave New World*, but it is of greatest concern to anthroposophists whose aim it is to increase the human potential for experience and develop body, soul and spirit to the fullest extent. As far as children are concerned this development of the personality in *all* its aspects can be achieved with practically no pressure on the part of the teacher.

Steiner is supposed to have said that there are but three effective agents in education: compulsion, ambition and love, and then to have added simply: "We do without the first two".

A Social Education

This statement will be met with blank incredulity on the part of many a product of conventional schooling. For we have come to believe that competition is one of the basic fundamentals of existence. The struggle for survival characterises nature, and competition is essential for the working of a successful economy. Both these statements are only partly true. The vast majority of cultures have been based on co-operation and not on competition. Japan's recent enormous industrial advance was achieved in a climate of remarkably little competition.[4]

In education too competition has only a limited value. It enables people to win a prize, a special place in class, excellent marks. But the subject studied is thereby degraded and becomes merely the means by which such achievements are accomplished. In a Steiner school the subject stands in the centre of interest and the intention of the teacher, as we have already seen, is to interest and involve his pupils in what is being studied. To this end one has to approach one's subject from a variety of points so that all one's pupils are able to connect to it. Each one can bring some individual contributions and the class will but be enriched by their variety. One of the most joyful experiences of the author, who spent his working life in one of the British Steiner schools, was to be able to watch how his more intelligent pupils valued their less endowed classmates. They had learned to appreciate the practical, moral, athletic or artistic gifts of others and enjoyed the riches of human diversity that made up their class. So a sense of respect for the individual was engendered, human relationships fostered and co-operation on a large scale achieved, lessons of the greatest value for a happier social future.

The Proof of the Pudding

Steiner schools are unstreamed and they do not quantify their pupils' progress. How can one compare their achievements to those of more orthodox establishments? Teachers in Steiner schools have always insisted that the only fair way would be to compare the adult lives of their former pupils with a corresponding group from other scholastic systems: to compare their achievements, but not only these. What are the respective contributions of the two groups to the furtherance of social relationships? What about their involvement in public affairs? What is the social value of their work? Do they differ in their ability to come to terms with themselves and find fulfilment in their lives? Possible indicators in response to the last question might be the number of suicides, the stability of marriages, the record of physical and mental health. As far as we are aware no such comprehensive research has been carried out.

The German government, however, which to a considerable extent finances German Steiner schools, carried out an enquiry into the question of relative achievement. In the late seventies researchers investigated the careers of pupils in two classes of two different Steiner schools who had completed their schooling twenty years previously. Their careers and present positions were compared to those of other school leavers in the same two towns and of the same socio-economic background. The result of the investigation is in print[5] and confirms that even in terms of *achievement* the pupils of the unstreamed Steiner schools had performed better in a modern, competitive society than had their contemporaries who in their school days had been subjected to constant marking and competition.

Curative Work

It cannot be the purpose of this study to look in depth at every aspect of anthroposophical work. What we were able to say about the arts and education dealt only with a few principal concerns and did not go into any detail. Even less will be said about other spheres of work. A few indications about the most important must suffice. Outstanding is the work with handicapped children and adults which, particularly in Britain, has been given a good deal of recognition. It is generally felt that anthroposophists are second to none in their ability to create a truly therapeutic environment and to take the handicapped adult or child into the totality of their lives. Artists and doctors, teachers and craftsmen, farmers, therapists and others combined to give handicapped children the possibility to unfold the kernel of their being in spite of the limitations of their handicap, and to create for handicapped adults an environment in which they can live fulfilled lives. Co-workers feel that in these people an eternal individuality is present, of equal standing to their own. However, in the mysterious fashion in which human karma works, physical obstacles stand in the way of this individuality developing his or her full potential during this particular life on earth. There are a number of books which describe this work in greater detail.[6]

Medicine

It is, of course, impossible for a layman to explain the intricacies of a school of medicine. One or two aspects of the work in an anthroposophical hospital have already been pointed out. Anthroposophical doctors can call on the diagnostic and therapeutic resources available to their non-anthroposophical colleagues, but in addition have at their disposal a wide variety of specially prepared medicines, some of them based on definite indications by Steiner. New laboratory procedures help to establish a diagnostic picture. Wherever the state of the patient permits a choice the anthroposophical doctor will forego drugs which drastically interfere with the normal working of the organism and will aim at increasing the self-healing, regenerative forces in the patient he is treating.

Agriculture

Since 1924 anthroposophists have worked farms, orchards, gardens and forests in an ecologically acceptable way. Their method is called *biodynamic*. Together with other ways of organic farming it refuses to work with artificial manure, poison sprays and other products of the chemical industry. The farm is experienced not as a means of money-making or dodge for taxable income, but as a part of the planet whose life has to be preserved for our health and that of succeeding generations. The biodynamic method uses organic preparations in homeopathic dilutions which are to preserve and strengthen the inherent fertility of the soil and to bring cosmic influences into play which will increase the nutritive value of agricultural products. Special care is taken to make each farm or market garden an integrated whole which easily fits into the ecology of its natural surroundings and still has its own individual nature. The farmer sees himself as a servant: a servant to the soil, to his fellow men for whom he prepares healthy and nourishing food, and to future generations. Special financial and marketing arrangements have often to be made to enable him to perform his service.

A Summary

We have looked mainly at two different spheres of activity, the arts and education, in our effort to show how anthroposophists quite spontaneously connect their insights into man and world with their daily lives. Many of them feel that anthroposophy is not something in addition to their ordinary lives, but *is* their life in all its aspects. Like Marxists they are concerned not only with reflection on what has already occurred, but also with the active shaping of the future. This was recognised in a charming and perceptive article by Joseph Huber, a German Marxist.[7] We Marxists, he says, are famous dreamers, but when we descend into reality and want to achieve a certain practical alternative we come up against the anthroposophist who says: "Sorry, chap, I have already done what you have been dreaming about." Huber then goes on to exemplify this statement: "Here is a classless hospital, there a special co-operative bank, there are autonomous kindergartens and schools, publishing houses, alternative therapeutic and medical centres, free art academies, laboratories producing medicines, biodynamic farms and other institutions. Where today's Left makes a big noise and achieves relatively little, anthroposophists are quietly building up a lot . . . These and other institutions together with their countless sympathisers in ordinary institutions form a kind of informal multi-national concern which is active in science, art and architecture, in economic, financial and organisational consultancies, and in agriculture, the distribution of food and in health and education services . . . Without having to hide the anthroposophical movement is much better integrated within the existing system and among widely different groups of people, and outside this system it has, through its own institutions, a far higher degree of independence than any alternative grouping. This is not so much the cause, but one consequence of a successful activity."

This summary reflects the fact that in some European countries anthroposophy is becoming a distinct part of the respective national cultures and is seen as a viable alternative to our shallow and materialist civilisation. At present this is hardly the case in English-speaking countries.

A last glance at the activities described above. They are practical and workable. They all focus on a common factor: man. He is taken seriously as a being of body, soul and spirit and around the resultant needs the 'new world' is shaped. Certain intentions common to all these activities have become clear: to set people free, to increase the dignity and riches of human existence, to encourage man's creativity and responsibility, to learn to co-operate and to heal. These features will be studied further in the next chapter.

Chapter Eight
Social Renewal

Rudolf Steiner's intentions for social renewal deserve a chapter on their own. Not only are they basic for all outer work done by anthroposophists, they also deserve a special place in his biography in as much as he began to articulate these intentions almost twenty years before he started on his work as a teacher of the spirit. They are also one of three areas which belong uniquely to Steiner, the other two being the concrete, detailed research into karmic relationships, and his insistence on autonomous man, a being alone responsible for his decisions and his morality, the future ally of the gods. About all other areas, practical, spiritual, existential he spoke when he was specifically asked, these three concerns he put forward on his own, – and found little or no response among the theosophists and, later, even among those who gathered around him to form the Anthroposophical Society of 1913.

We said above that Steiner's social intentions are basic to all practical activities carried out in his name. Unfortunately, this fact has not always been realised, and even today there exist places which continue to work in his name, but with outworn social practices. This is understandable. Steiner, the teacher of freedom, did not press his sensitivities and insights on those with whom he worked. If they were unable to respond to his example, if they failed to read between the lines he would not insist, but co-operate with them within the boundaries they themselves set. Furthermore, many of the people who became particularly interested in his social ideas stressed their structural aspect, Threefolding, without seeing that this was only a *form* in which his social intentions found expression. It needed the example of people like Karl König, the founder of the Camphill Movement, and Dieter Brüll, Emeritus Professor of Law in the University of Amsterdam, to awaken us to the deeply Christian character of Steiner's social impulse. The former created therapeutic and social communities which practically manifested one way in which Steiner's intentions could be realised, the latter made a scholarly and exhaustive study of these intentions[1] which are scattered throughout Steiner's work, sometimes worked out in some detail, sometimes simply as hints or asides, sometimes recognisable only by the manner in which a particular problem is dealt with.

A Retrospect

In August 1922 Rudolf Steiner, at the invitation of certain British educationalists, gave at Oxford a course on his educational ideas.[2] He was asked to devote the last three days of his fortnight's stay to a discussion of social questions. These three lectures[3] are the last statement he was able to make on social problems and, in a way, can be considered a retrospective summary of his social intentions. As such they are unique. But they are unique in another respect as well. It is the only time that Steiner developed his social intentions in front of a non-German-speaking audience. His ideas, he says to his British listeners, have been totally misunderstood. They constitute no utopia, no blueprint, no prescriptions, they are, at best, a model. They point a way in which social realities could be *gradually* transformed. How this transformation is to take place must depend on the actualities of a given time and place and on the social insights and sensitivities of the people concerned with this process of transformation, on their conscience and their consciousness.

What he himself had done, he continued, could only apply to one concrete situation, South West Germany in the midst of the political chaos following on the end of the German Empire. He had been asked by some industrialists of this region to put in print his ideas on what could and might be done there and then. These ideas were, however, no longer relevant to the German situation and never applied to the British scene. In Germany the state had taken control of most aspects of life. So it was necessary to tease apart the various strands of the social organism and ask where the boundaries of government control lay. Could there not be other bodies than the government to deal with the various spheres of society? So Steiner arrived at *Threefolding,* the process of establishing equivalent, but separate organs for the political, social and legal life of the country, for the economic activities and for the furtherance of cultural concerns, education, research, the arts, religion, etc.

Contemporaneously with Steiner the Guild Socialists advocated similar approaches in Britain. A few years later, Churchill contemplated the possibility of establishing three different assemblies in place of Parliament.

But in Britain things were different. At that time, in 1922, government had only begun to give directives to industry. The universities and, to a large extent, the whole school system were outside the confines of state intervention. Here, Steiner said, the problem was to *recognise* the separation of powers and to direct attention to the problem of *integration*. He did not go into any details in these three lectures, but by reference to other places we can easily see what this integration entailed. For example: how is a free educational system to be financed if it is to help, and not to harm, the socially disadvantaged? Is there a way other than government interference if we wish to stop employers from exploiting their labour force? Such questions were continuously in Steiner's mind and before long we shall turn our attention to them.

1917 - 1920: An Interlude

The attitude shown in these Oxford lectures seems at first to be at variance with the way Steiner acted in the years immediately before and after the end of the First World War. It has already been stated that against his usual habit he expounded in these years his social intentions *although* his Dornach audience would have preferred quite different subjects. But there were some people who reacted in a very positive way. These included men in positions of authority, foremost among them Count Otto Lerchenfeld, a Bavarian, and Count Ludwig Polzer-Holditz whose brother Arthur was *chef de cabinet* to the Emperor of Austria. In his reminiscences,[4] Count Arthur describes the impact a memorandum by Steiner addressed to the Austrian Emperor had made on him. He also saw the serious difficulties which it posed for the politicians. His first conversations with his brother, the anthroposophist, had left him in a sceptical frame of mind, but he wanted to examine the memorandum in detail, both for the intrinsic value of the thoughts expressed, as well as for their practicability.

Ten years after the event he summed up his reaction: "My impression was that this suggestion accounted completely for the practical needs of the immediate future, while the suggestions of others remained abstract. It seemed that the basic thoughts were generally right and that their realisation, however difficult, must be possible. But one would have needed the co-operation of a large part of humanity . . . Just because" these suggestions "stemmed from the world of the spirit and meant a final renunciation of traditional conditions and habits of thought I felt that they would be generally rejected. This was so particularly in 1917 when people mostly thought we would not have to drop too many traditional habits."⁰

Courage and imagination are not the usual characteristics of politicians, and neither in Austria nor in Germany did Steiner's ideas have any effect on the course of events.

The following years brought two new developments. A larger number of anthroposophists with experience in the economic and cultural fields became interested in Steiner's social ideas and were anxious to bring them to realisation. So Steiner was asked by industrialists in South West Germany to put down, in book form, his thoughts on social matters,⁶ others asked for a short statement of his aims, and successfully persuaded a few hundred prominent people to put their signatures to this appeal. The book was a reasonable success, but the appeal was of little consequence. However, Steiner met with real understanding when, again in South West Germany, he was given the opportunity to address the work-forces of some fairly large factories such as Waldorf-Astoria and Daimler. He had the ability to speak to workers in such a way that they could respond immediately. They felt they were not having theories or generalities thrown at them, but that here stood a man who could sense and express their unarticulated feelings and who offered new hope.

Steiner's success upset some of the petty trade union officials, and they prevented him from entering the factories. So Steiner's efforts had come to nothing: first, with the erstwhile rulers, then with the intelligentsia, and finally with the workers. For some time efforts continued to spread the new ideas and to re-organise a number of industrial and commercial undertakings. Later, Steiner presented some of his thoughts on economic and social matters in a more general manner.⁷ But his last words on the social question were spoken at Oxford. As we have seen, his intentions and his enthusiasm for social renewal had in no way abated.

Steiner strongly objected when his activities in the years 1917 to 1920 were considered *political*. But at first sight they seem just like that. He wrote memoranda, he gave lectures on topical themes, lectures to members, to the general public, to the work-forces of a number of medium-sized and large factories, he had discussions with politicians. What could he mean when he maintained that such activities were not political? The present writer believes that this question is relevant for an understanding of Steiner the man, and of his social intentions. There can be no doubt that he had an insight into the future of the twentieth century which far surpassed that of his contemporaries, particularly of politicians who hardly ever can see the wood for the trees. To deny these insights to others would have been negligent, almost criminally so. But he did not want any power for himself – very untypical for a politician – nor did he aspire to guiding the social situation into a particular mould. He pronounced certain insights, he suggested to the Austrian Emperor how an apparently hopeless situation could become fluid again, but when asked by enthusiastic workers what they should do he replied that this was for *them* to decide. Could Steiner, the teacher of freedom, have acted otherwise? He could not direct, lead or even persuade. He could but point out certain facts. He would advise, if and when a question came from a particular person who was qualified to act and would take full responsibility himself because he understood and was in agreement with Steiner's intentions.

Anti-Totalitarian, Anti-Nationalistic, Anti-Reich

With the benefit of the hindsight of two generations it is easy to see what Steiner aimed at: to establish in Central Europe a diversified social entity which by its example might mitigate the rigours of Western capitalism and Communist tyranny. His aim for Central Europe was threefold: he wanted to break down the power of the unitary state before it became completely totalitarian, he wanted to stem the intoxification of nationalism and to prevent the Germans from establishing another *Reich*. It is easy to imagine how much happier the destinies of Europe and the world would have been had Steiner found the right people to share his vision with him.

There are few people in the developed part of the world who would not happily subscribe to the idea of divesting government of many of its powers if only they could see this to be compatible with social justice. We shall later see how Steiner himself approached this problem but now we simply state that he – and the Guild Socialists as well as certain contemporary French socialists – realised that what is called State is an unholy alliance of powers which for the benefit of ordinary citizens had much better be disentangled into three semi-independent organisms. Each of the three would function according to its own inherent laws, and we, the ordinary citizens, would be involved in all three. Government would, on a democratic basis, deal with the rights of men, in other words would establish priorities and set certain boundaries. Supposing that such an aim could be gradually realised we would witness a tremendous decrease of pressure on us and an increasing sense of liberation and individual responsibility. Instead of this the Germans experienced totalitarianism to an extreme degree, as did Eastern Europe in a somewhat different form, while the once-free West continues to build up an ever-increasing bureaucracy which shares its power with big business. The latter, equally powerful, if not more so, constantly creates new facts which are beyond any democratic control, but more than anything else shape the life of our civilisation.

Equally, Steiner set himself against nationalism, and in particular against the nation state. We see in, say, Switzerland and the United Kingdom that it is possible for different national cultures to co-exist under common government. Steiner's idea that the political and cultural entities need not necessarily share the same boundaries might have prevented the apparently insoluble tragedy of Northern Ireland. In 1917/8 Steiner was possibly the only articulate person who saw the hollowness of Woodrow Wilson's slogan of *The Freedom of Nations*. Freedom, Steiner held, pertains to individuals, and not to nations. It is a function of the way I am governed and not of the language the tax collector speaks. Wilson's idea, of course, never worked. The peace treaties of 1919 only multiplied the problem and today there exists a Congress of European Minorities which consists apparently of over 200 different minorities, each with their own grievances. Steiner wanted to preserve Austria-Hungary as a *political* entity, but break the cultural dominance of the German-speaking population in the one half of the country and the even stronger dominance of the Magyars in the other. Had he succeeded, the peoples of Central and Eastern Europe might have been spared the attention of Hitler and, later, of Stalin.

In the decisive years after the defeat of Germany and its allies Steiner addressed himself mainly to Germans. For so radical a social renewal as he had in mind the shock of defeat, the shattering of illusions and the general social chaos provided a helpful basis. Steiner's endeavour was to show Germans that the pursuit of the idea of the *Reich*, a centre of political dominance in the heart of Europe, could but be destructive. He tried to make Germans realise that they could only influence the world if they concentrated on what was universally human. All through his life he pointed to the enormous cultural treasures which Germans could call their own, in particular to Goethe and Novalis. Such men, however, concerned themselves with what is universally human and so transcended what is purely German. If Germans were able to incorporate the insights of such people into their national life they would transform it to their own benefit, to the benefit of Europe and of the world.

Such attitudes made Steiner a target for German nationalists and they made an attempt on his life. As a result he stopped lecturing in public to German audiences and repeatedly warned that if "these gentlemen" were to assume power in Germany this would be tantamount to the downfall of Germany and put an end to his hopes for the humanising influence of Goethe and the Goetheanists.

Today, it seems all but obvious that Steiner was bound to fail in such a gigantic attempt at social renewal, particularly as he would never countenance any but peaceful means. Why, then, should he have given so large a slice of his time and energy to this endeavour? We have already stated our opinion that not to act on his far-reaching insights would have been cowardly and irresponsible. A true Christian, he believed in the power of transformation. He had taught in his *Philosophy of Freedom* that moral intuitions, to be of any value to others, had to be realised gradually and with full consideration of all the people involved in this transformation. If, on the other hand, such an insight or intuition does not affect the social scene it becomes abstract and dead. What the social reality can bear, how much it is capable of transformation can never be decided intellectually and in advance. So he felt the attempt had to be made. Today the number of people who have seen the sinister sides of nationalism, state power and the influence of the multinational firms has grown. They, even today, might find inspiration in Steiner's attempt two generations ago.

Individual Freedom and Responsibility

We now turn away from this dramatic and tragedy-laden interlude in order to uncover the roots of Steiner's social intentions. We arrive there at two convictions which, at first, seem incompatible with each other. Both are, however, deeply anchored in Steiner's total awareness of man and his destiny. To put the first conviction concisely: In the early stages of man's development – we might call it the tribal state – the individual served the needs of the community. His role within it was clearly defined, although in the course of a lifetime a man was quite likely to play a succession of roles. But today, the community ought to serve the needs of the individual and it is for the individual to decide what part in the social whole he wants to play. There is no doubt that, by and large, this development is a historical fact. Steiner thus denies the modern community the right to prescribe to the individual what he is to do. Today, we find it degrading if 'the state' – in other words, officialdom – tells us what career we may or may not pursue, whether we may or may not travel abroad, what we should think, read or wear. Modern man, Steiner holds, will only flourish where there is no uniformity, no pressure from on high, where thoughts are free and creativity unfettered. This attitude is, of course, connected to Steiner's basic conviction that modern man must consciously learn to increase his sphere of responsibility, to learn to live out of his own spiritual resources so that he approaches his overriding task to become an ally of the Divine Powers, to develop from the Son of God to the Son of Man.

Industry and Alienation

Steiner's conviction of the autonomy of the individual will be shared by many contemporaries. But his other conviction may cause surprise. Not because it is illogical or flies in the face of facts, it simply happens that this train of thought is unfamiliar to most. Not so long ago people of a conservative outlook could point to the life of a Scottish crofter or Alpine farmer as an almost ideal situation: the man and his family were self-sufficient, they produced all they needed, they mainly consumed what they themselves had produced. Or they might point to another ideal of self-sufficiency: the feudal estate. There a much wider variety of goods was produced, but people were still able to understand the social purpose of their labour and identify with the work they were doing. Such situations were contrasted with the lot of the factory worker, alienated from the fruits of his work. The result of such comparisons was regret and condemnation of industrialisation.

Steiner, who knew the life of a manual worker from first-hand experience, had no wish to go back to a supposed ideal. While he was in no way inclined to acquiesce in, or condone the conditions in which the industrial worker found himself at the beginning of this century, he realised that industrial development increased the realm of discretion and autonomy of more and more people, that it *could* be a powerful agent on the way towards freedom, and that it was a good thing to produce for others and not just for oneself and one's family. He was among the first who realised that modern industry had built a global net of interdependence, that what happened in one country economically affected the rest of the world, that it was illogical to think of economic questions in any but global terms. The more clearly we recognise these facts the greater our ability to work in the realm of economics not in competition with each other, but more like brothers.

Human Rights

So we arrive at two fundamentally different systems, one of cultural activities – art, religion, education, etc. – and one of economic activities, comprising production of goods and services, distribution and consumption. The former tends towards anarchy, the latter, when not aware of the inherent proclivity of mutual service and brotherhood, towards large organisational structures likely to lead to the exploitation of the economically weakest and to the development of immense power outside any democratic control. A third realm, that of human rights, of equity, is, however, able to transform the socially destructive sides of the other two spheres and to integrate all into an organism in which the various functions are recognised, allowed their independent ways of working, but learn to harmonise their activities.

Social, Moral, Spiritual

Before we look at some practical details we shall now consider this idea of *Threefolding* within the totality of Steiner's work. It is not an addition to the work of a teacher of the spirit, but is deeply rooted in his total awareness of the world. It is deeply Christian, both in its insistence on the freedom of the individual and in its readiness to accept totally the fact of human interdependence. In the social field this means making my neighbour's needs the motivation for my action, and in the moral field to help my brother to bear his cross. It must have been one of the most disappointing occurrences in Steiner's life that very few of his friends managed to see the underlying unity between his spiritual insights and the activities which to them seemed 'political' and therefore of little importance.

Capitalism and Socialism

By now it must have become obvious that Steiner's social intentions are incompatible with the ethos of capitalism. Its basis is the naive belief that competition is 'natural' whereas in reality the majority of societies known to us were based on co-operation and not on competition. By measuring every human activity by its degree of profitability capitalism destroyed not only our environment, but also the cohesion of society and the morality of the individual. It set one man against the other and encouraged us to be mean, aggressive and grabbing. But Steiner most of all attacked the hallowed principle of the play of market forces. In a lecture in Vienna in April 1914 he called this principle a cancer in our society which threatened to destroy us. As he later repeatedly stated, he meant this as a warning of the war which within a few months was to engulf the whole of Europe.

Although Steiner had much sympathy with certain tendencies towards a more socialist structure of society he could not but violently disagree with Marx's prescriptions. These were bound to increase the power of an anonymous bureaucracy and jeopardise the free initiative of the 'people on the spot'.

Some of Steiner's Constraints

Perhaps we can now realise some of the extraordinary constraints under which Steiner had to operate. He could but appeal to the free insight of people, but there were not many free people around. Most of his followers looked to him for leadership, but he believed that the social situation had to be changed by the people on the spot, not by somebody like himself who realised the need for action, but stood outside the actual situation. In his lectures and writings he refused to go into detail in order to leave people free, in his addresses he refused for the same reason to persuade and stir up emotions. A good idea of how he acted in these circumstances are the six lectures in Zürich on *The Social Future*.[8] There he went into greater detail than he did usually, possibly because in this rich and fairly untroubled city the chances of practical consequences of his talks seemed remoter than in Germany where radical change was one of the possibilities of the social scene.

In the previous chapter we did not go into much practical detail, mainly because there exist good introductions to other activities based on Steiner's thoughts. However, there is no comprehensive introduction in English to Steiner's social ideas. So it seems reasonable to indicate the direction in which Steiner would have wished things to develop.

Three Radical Goals

Two examples will have to suffice. The economic sphere was to deal with production, distribution and consumption. Through this definition three areas were taken outside the confines of economic activity: land, labour and money. Like the Guild Socialists, Steiner realised that the buying of labour was not so far removed from buying the whole person, that *wagery* is but a variant of slavery. Those familiar with the history of the Industrial Revolution will realise that the former was not always gentler than the latter. In 1919 Steiner's ideas seemed utopian or revolutionary. Today, millions of Europeans – pensioners, invalids, unemployed – receive an income which is not related to what they are doing at this moment. The logic of facts urged such an arrangement on a society which, essentially, is still shaped by the assumptions of capitalism. Much better, if the whole question had been debated in a comprehensive way, if it had in no way been given the flavour of charitable action but had simply been discussed under the heading: what are the needs of men of today? A question for the democratic rights sphere to discuss. Then, of course, the next thing would have to be negotiations between representatives of the political and economic spheres whether and how these needs could be met. Equally radical is Steiner's view on the ownership of land. We who are heirs to Roman ideas of ownership believe, almost instinctively, that every piece of land must have an owner. Other civilisations had different ideas. Land belonged to the king or the temple or to the ancestors. The *use* of land was entrusted, possibly within certain limits, to identifiable people or, in earlier times to a village community or a tribe. The result of our ideas of ownership is that land can be bought or sold as if it had the character of goods, that is objects produced by man. Land becomes an object of speculation. Without any effort on the part of the owner it can increase its value tenfold. In the last twenty years there has been a phenomenal rise in land values which contributed substantially to the rate of inflation. This rise was rarely discussed on its merits or otherwise, but was simply taken as something unavoidable, 'in the nature of things'. Steiner would encourage arrangements which would enable suitably qualified people to *use* land. If we applied this principle to agricultural land we could see to it that only people with experience in farming could be land users. With the enormous capital costs for land gone we could insist on preservation of the quality of soil, on respect for the ecology of the place and on safeguards for the future. Paradoxical as it may sound, money too is taken out of the sphere of economics. Like land it has not the character of man-produced goods. It is seen as a kind of lubricant in the economic process which facilitates the production of and distribution of goods. But it is not a thing in itself, it exists only in relation to the goods produced. If allowed an autonomous life it is likely to cause grave social problems. It encourages social irresponsibility. Our present arrangements allow skilled manipulators of money an enormous amount of power which is subject to few democratic controls. The whole economy of a country can be gravely affected by the way people with no concern for the country speculate in the international money markets.

Here too Steiner would distinguish between *use* and *ownership*, this time not of land, but of capital. He indicated a number of ways in which money could become the instrument to enable men to work freely and creatively in economic life. In present circumstances money, too often, acts as an instrument of power and a means of enslavement. Also in this respect the logic of facts has moved in the direction that Steiner wanted to go consciously: today it is very much easier to *use* money which is not ours – we call this *credit* – than it was in Steiner's time. By proceeding pragmatically we increased the power of banks. Had we entered into a discussion of the principle involved we might have realised that here would have been a lever to bring about vast, and socially healthy changes in the structure of our society and in our motivation in business and industry. Hardly any progress has been made in limiting the *ownership* of capital. Death duties and capital gains tax are some rather isolated and tentative measures. The result has been the amassing of large capital sums in the hands of individuals or, even more so, of anonymous corporations. To what extent these sums were applied to the social welfare of the society whose work and interrelationships enabled these financial gains to be made must remain a matter of conjecture.

We can now look back. Steiner would encourage the breaking of the link between work and income, would ensure that the needs of all are covered and would limit the power of individuals to act in a socially irresponsible way by taking land, labour and capital out of the realm of economics. The cost of labour would be determined by democratic means, the access to the use of land and capital would be regulated by duly qualified persons. This would enable people with imagination, creativity and responsibility to engage in industry and agriculture. Profitability would be only *one* factor in these enterprises.

In Place of the Market

The capitalist believes in the validity of the law of supply and demand. It is 'natural' and it works to the good of us all. As a matter of fact, it does not work. A simple example from Britain: A generation ago we could buy a good variety of inks. Then a certain American firm offered to supply retailers with modern counters, illuminated from within, on condition that the particular retailer concentrated on the products of this firm. Within a short time most inks disappeared from the shops in spite of the demand for them not having decreased. If today I want to buy a fountain pen with cartridges the firm in question supplies one set of cartridges 'free', in other words they sell the pen *and* the cartridges in one operation. But if I prefer to use a different colour of ink than the firm deems right I shall have to pay for a second set of cartridges made by the same firm. The firm is not interested in my *demand*, it *supplies* what is best for the firm. The competition was eliminated a generation ago. True enough, there is a second firm supplying pens and inks. How does the customer know whether this is in reality one firm trading under two different names, two firms owned by the same holding company, or two genuinely independent firms? A harmless example. But once we look a bit more critically at the realities of business methods today we shall see that neither is there a genuine relationship between demand and supply, nor does market research find out what the customer really needs, but only in what guise the firm can best sell their product. Few firms genuinely strive to achieve a healthy relationship between themselves and their customers, most have only one aim: to maximise their profits. The idea of the *market* deciding what goods shall be produced and at what price is but fiction. The reality is vastly different.

Steiner insists that economic life is to serve the actual needs of the customer. This would inject a totally different motivation into industry than the maximisation of profit. What these needs in fact are can only be established without the confines of the state, and only through real and open discussion. Lately we have often heard 'management is here to manage'. Steiner thinks the opposite: Business is here to serve. Of course, the manager has to have wide discretion. How else could he function imaginatively and creatively? How else could society expect to attract men of quality into industry? But the overall management of industry would lie in the hands of *Associations*. These would be of various kinds, but their general principle would be meeting places of opposites, producers, distributors and consumers, management, work force and planners, representatives of the the shoe industry and of the suppliers of leather, plastic materials and canvas, etc. In such discussions would be established both the kind of goods to be produced and the fair price at which they are to be sold. In present circumstances it might be difficult to envisage that real and open discussions would be feasible and produce any tangible results. But just in this respect anthroposophists have acquired considerable experience as we shall mention below.

A Realistic Assessment

Steiner's ideas can in many respects appear more unconventional than communism. Perhaps they really are. Not only is a radical reorganisation of industrial relationships, of questions of ownership and of the role of money intended, but the amount of personal responsibility and discretion of each citizen would be greatly increased. Is such a change feasible, a new change which would presuppose new attitudes and motivations? Originally, anthroposophists believed such a change could be introduced at a stroke, either by decree from above or through the impetus generated by a powerful, largely proletarian movement. Today, this is seen as illusory. Those who today take seriously Steiner's social intentions try to adapt and develop them. They have mainly three aims: to help to humanise and gradually change existing institutions, to be ready in case a wider reform would be necessary after a possible social cataclysm, and meanwhile to set up small and medium-sized organisations which can provide material for social studies and serve as models for future and larger activities. A few of the activities at present in being shall be mentioned here: banks which foster a conscious and social use of money, income communities where, say, a dozen members of different financial standing pool their income, consumer organisations which guarantee the livelihood of one or more ecologically working farmers, an international group of institutes for organisation development. This group – one of these in the U.K. bears the significant name of Transform – study and give advice on problems in the development of medium and large-scale organisations. They have learned a good deal about the solution of conflicts, about genuine discussions between various interests and different personalities in the same organisation, and about reaching a consensus about the aims and methods of particular firms. Such knowledge will be invaluable if and when the first associations which Steiner envisaged come into being.

Chapter Nine
The Anthroposophical Society

In the first chapter of this book we referred in one paragraph to the foundation of the General Anthroposophical Society at Christmas 1923. (See *The Anthroposophical Society*.) This foundation can be looked at from many aspects, and in particular we might mention here a book by Rudolf Grosse[1] which treats this subject within its wider setting. We are concerned here at first with two questions: What caused Steiner, then 62 years old, to found this society so late in life, and, is such a society really necessary? Only then shall we turn to the particular features which distinguish the Society.

Rudolf Steiner in 1923

1923 had begun with disaster: the wooden double dome of the first Goetheanum, this unique manifestation of Steiner's spiritual impulse, had been destroyed by arson. The loss of this building on which such high hopes had been put, on which, for ten years, such devoted work had been spent, could easily have shattered a younger man. For Steiner it meant a thorough re-examination of his work, of his own position, of his aims and methods, and from this sprang an entirely new phase of his work, perhaps the most glorious. It centred in the foundation of the Anthroposophical Society.

Already before he had suffered many times from the weaknesses of his followers, their traditionalism, their narrow-mindedness, their dogmatism, their dissensions: "Since 1912, particularly since 1918 my real intentions were constantly blunted by the Society." (Konstitution, p.105). As he now surveyed the scene and hoped for some new impulse to arise from among the members he was confronted by a feeling of helplessness and lack of responsible initiatives. He met violent disagreements between old and young, a lack of tolerance, a love of hierarchy and of authoritative demands. If there was to be a new society it was he who had to found it. Only in this way could a society arise which guaranteed individual freedom without which no spiritual life as he experienced it could flourish.

Anthroposophy without an Anthroposophical Society

But, we may ask ourselves, is there any need for an Anthroposophical Society at all? Surely, I can study Steiner's work very well on my own? Surely, if what we have said so far in this book gives a true account of Steiner's intentions there is no need for a centralised authority for any practical activity based on his work? Is not each institution self-governing? People who feel the impulse and are backed by a number of interested friends have opened schools, clinics, laboratories. Others might publish anthroposophical literature, others still arrange public lectures. Is there any reason for a society?

But without a society we shall miss the experience of "the two or three gathered together in His name". Such a gathering cannot be goal-directed, say called together to discuss problems concerning a particular Steiner school. If this is to be in *His* name it will be a meeting of *free* individuals each aware of his own spiritual entity and that of all others 'gathered together'. The Christian character of Anthroposophy needs a society with its appropriate social life. Such a society Steiner offered to his friends. Here, at last, he was able to realise his social intentions, – at least, ideally. At first, members of the new society rarely realised the unique character of the society they had joined, and so Steiner's creation remained incomplete. But as the understanding of his social intentions grew the Society began to manifest its inherent features more and more. So it is a truly exciting task for anybody who feels committed to Steiner to work within the Society which he founded and help to mould it according to the intentions of its founder. That there are other reasons for joining the Society will, we hope, become apparent in the course of this chapter.

A Society without Opinions

The most outstanding feature of this society is the fact that the new entrant is not asked to subscribe to any opinion or programme and does not pledge himself to carry out any obligations. He is free, he has not changed his opinions, has not been converted to a set of beliefs nor has he adopted a new form of life. His opinions are his own. He cannot hold heterodox views as there is no institutionalised orthodoxy.

Conversely, neither the Anthroposophical Society in Great Britain nor the General Anthroposophical Society in Dornach can make any pronouncements in the name of their members. Whatever opinions the President of the Society may hold, say on the rights and wrongs of a European Confederation, on nuclear energy or the existence and activity of angels, – and he may hold very definite ideas – he cannot express them on behalf of the members of the Society. Neither can he make those opinions binding on others. He is free to voice his own opinions, but so is every member. This means that there cannot be any centralised direction, whether from Dornach or from any regional grouping, and so each member as well as each individual institution within the movement is alone responsible for their actions. Consequently, life in the Society is stimulating and challenging. It offers enormous opportunities for practising new forms of social relationships where widely different people with widely different views learn to respect and work with each other. This task all but defeated the first generation of anthroposophists.

A Common Impulse

If opinions do not hold the Anthroposophical Society together, what does? It is the discovery of a common impulse which makes the newcomer wish to join the Society. He might have gone to hear a public lecture or seen a performance of eurythmy, he might have had a conversation with a friend who happened to be an anthroposophist, he might have worked for a certain time at a Steiner school. He now realises that a common motivation inspires the people he met, and gradually he sees that this common motivation has its origin in certain spiritual experiences. These may be subconscious, stemming from pre-natal events, which karmically helped to shape the present earth life, but they may also be cultivated by conscious meditative practice. If the newcomer can feel that the common impulse in the people he has met is also present in him, if he can joyfully respond to what motivates the others he will think of these people no longer as 'them', but as 'us'. The way into the Society will now be open to him.

This spiritual fact is described by Steiner in the fourth paragraph of the 'Statutes' he proposed for the Anthroposophical Society. (He had first pointed out that these were no prescriptive statutes, but a *description* of human realities.) – Membership of the Society is open to all regardless of nation, class or religion, but also regardless of scientific or artistic convictions – i.e. opinions – "who see something justifiable in the existence of such an institution as the Goetheanum in Dornach as a Free School of the Science of the Spirit." The reader might contemplate the choice of words used. *Justifiable* and *such as* make it abundantly clear that no exclusive claims and no authoritative demands are made. *School of the Science of the Spirit* will be explained below. The sentence in its totality manifests a deep seriousness as well as a truly amazing spiritual freedom. It points to the most intimate concern of all who can truly call themselves anthroposophists.

The School

Within the Anthroposophical Society Steiner instituted a school which was to lead, in definite steps, the anthroposophical student to an ever-increasing awareness of spiritual realities. The aim of this schooling is not to estrange the pupil from life. On the contrary, the strengthening and clarifying of his inner experience will help him to play a more responsible and conscious part in his personal life and in the work which he is engaged in. He will not *know* more than other anthroposophists nor will he gain in power, but the schooling will help him to let flow into every aspect of his life the fruits of his experience in his meditative efforts and discipline.

Steiner did not allow everybody into this School. A certain condition had to be met and an undertaking given. The condition was familiarity with anthroposophical ways – a two years' membership of the Society was thought necessary in most cases. – Also the new entrant was expected to feel himself a true representative of Anthroposophy, somebody ready and able to stand by the Society, defend it when under attack and care for the quality of life within it. He was further expected to work in a collegial manner with other members of the School who were engaged in the same sphere of work as he, for instance in farming. Beyond this he remained as free as anybody else, no other demands being made upon him.

It might not be amiss to note here that the prerequisites for any meditative work on Steiner's lines, good health, physically and mentally, hold good also in connection with the School.

Steiner had hoped that the results of the meditative work of members of the School would irradiate every aspect of the Society so that anybody coming in contact with the latter would feel an unusual atmosphere of human concern, human understanding and spirituality. Two generations later we cannot say that the aim he had in mind has been achieved, though there are not a few occasions when the Society *is* what he meant it to be. There is, of course, man's fallibility, a subject about which we may have more to say in the final chapter. But there is also the fact that Steiner died before he could complete the School, and give sufficient indications for the way he visualised its working. Against this, there remains the undeniable fact that many people experienced through this School the reality of the spirit as others could only experience it *face to face* with a spiritual teacher living in the flesh.

The Society as a Training Ground

The General Anthroposophical Society was the only sphere which, in principle at least, Steiner was able to shape according to his social intentions. The two poles, freedom of the autonomous individual and the willing cooperation of these individuals, which underlie Steiner's social impulse, permeate the life of the Society. Each of these attitudes is difficult to achieve. Most of us look for precedents, tradition and convention instead of acting responsibly and creatively ourselves. Most of us are happy to obey, – especially if we in turn can command others. To shape one's actions in constant relationship with a partner or partners is much more difficult. To achieve a creative tension between these two poles is an even greater undertaking. But on this ground the life of the Society stands, "for in mutual give and take in spiritual matters human life unfolds its truest essence."[2] This give and take applies to people holding very different opinions, but "he who would be a true member should strive in the deepest places of his soul for inner tolerance"[3] towards his colleagues and fellow members. The same attitude applies to relations between centre and periphery. The life of the Society is not built on pronouncements from the centre. What the member can expect from the centre is initiatives. "But you know for the blood circulation you need not only centrifugal forces, but also those which work centripetally".[4] Communications are to flow in both directions. Steiner did not want members to join the General Anthroposophical Society directly, but through a group of a regional anthroposophical society, say the York Group of the Anthroposophical Society in Great Britain. "As a general rule every member should join a group. Only those who find it quite impossible to enter a group should apply for admission to Dornach as individual members."[5] Within such a group the give and take of Society life can take place and the reality and importance of human relationships within the Society can be experienced. Without such a group the study of anthroposophy can become academic and sterile. Within it can reach moments of almost religious intensity. Groups can form in many different ways and not only on a local or regional basis. "It is not by uniformity, but by variety that we shall reach the goal of the Anthroposophical Society."[6] Each group has a distinct life of its own and therefore will give itself, if members wish it, its own statutes, provided they do not contradict the Statutes of the General Anthroposophical Society.

The foundation of the Anthroposophical Society in 1923 was, in one respect, no more than a beginning. Steiner gave members a body, the soul of which was to be the School, but the life of which had to be created by him and all the members. This life cannot be created by command, it can only flow from free decisions of the members of the Society. Those who wish to unite themselves with this Society do in the hope that they, together with others, can make this life a reality and so work out of Steiner's social and spiritual impulses, the importance of which for the future history of mankind they have freely understood and affirmed for themselves.

Chapter Ten
Ways to Rudolf Steiner – and Obstacles

Owen Barfield might be known to some non-anthroposophists, both from his own works and from C. S. Lewis's autobiography *Surprised by Joy*. There Lewis describes his lifelong friendship with Barfield and the correspondence they had about the validity of Anthroposophy. This correspondence they called *The Great War*. It is the subject of a very instructive book by Lionel Adey[1] in which Professor Adey describes his hesitation to come to grips with Steiner whom he finds hard going. (This is the second book by a North American academic who treats Barfield with great understanding while in his own country his work is often overlooked.) – "Nevertheless, as any serious Blake scholar must read Swedenborg, so a student of Barfield's thought, or even Lewis's, must grit his teeth and read at least those works by Steiner that Barfield had read at the time of *The Great War*."[2] What is true of Professor Adey is also true of many other people with less well trained minds: Steiner *is* difficult and the difficulty is increased for people living in the totally different social and intellectual climate of the English-speaking world three generations after Steiner.

But why should Rudolf Steiner *want* to be difficult? It certainly is not that he *cannot* put clearly and simply what he has to say. Among the many examples that could be quoted for simplicity of diction we only mention here the *Lectures to Workmen*[3], the men who worked at the Goetheanum building and who asked him to answer some of their questions. There are at least two reasons which made Steiner *choose* a difficult form of presentation. To approach spiritual realities cannot be a hobby to be indulged in on Sundays. To be the pupil of an authentic Eastern sage is a full-time occupation. No true teacher, wherever he lived, ever pretended that barring special karmic circumstances or Divine grace access to spiritual insight was easy to achieve. On the contrary, at many schools of wisdom, including some Christian monastic orders, would-be entrants were severely warned and were admitted only after they had proved their eagerness and persistence. This attitude of warning off is enhanced, in Steiner's case, by his continuous insistence on the freedom of the other. So no attempt is made at persuasion, at influencing the reader emotionally, at prettifying the aspect of reality described. The treatment of the subject matter in hand is as cool and objective as possible, 'scientific' as it was called in Steiner's time. Some anthroposophists were from the beginning encouraged by Steiner's austere and demanding style. Many more had to overcome their initial frustration and make – as Steiner had intended – a real effort to penetrate his lectures and, particularly, his books.

This objectivity brings a danger with it. Spiritual facts objectively described may easily seem to be like physical facts. The specifically inward dimension is in danger of being lost in the presentation. To prevent this mistaken attitude in his students Steiner uses formulations which are designed to take off the hard edge of words, to bring into flow what is static, to focus on a fact simultaneously from more than one vantage point, comparable to the manner of Braque and Picasso in painting. This style increases the demands made on the student both of the original German and of English translations.

So how can we approach Rudolf Steiner?

Personal Contact

Perhaps the easiest approach to anthroposophy is living among, and working with, anthroposophists. This will, of course, tell the newcomer not very much about Steiner's teaching, but a very great deal about imponderables: values, prejudices, idiosyncracies, motivation, individual differences, human relationships. By and by the newcomer will feel to what an extent he can identify with the life that goes on around him and will discover whether, existentially, he 'belongs' to this place and to the whole movement that gave it shape. Three possible pitfalls have to be faced: that first impressions can deceive and that only a longer stay in the particular community can bring clarity, that the faults of individuals should not be blamed on Rudolf Steiner, and that living in a community may teach one very little about the details of Steiner's researches in any particular area. So one may have only the haziest idea of what anthroposophy speaks about while one spends one's active life doing work in the name of Steiner. The newcomer may take on instinctively certain attitudes and opinions prevailing in the particular community and so fail to aspire to the state of independence and free decision so essential to Steiner's ideal of modern man unless life in the community is accompanied by independent study and inquiry.

In this way, however, the newcomer can approach anthroposophy on more than one level. In his own study he can come to grips with Steiner's work while the community will show him some of the social and practical consequences of this work. He will also, most likely, find one or more persons with whom he can discuss the problems which arise in the course of his studies. The possibility for such conversations with, at least, one trusted friend is most valuable. It is almost a necessity but, obviously, it does not require a whole community, this service can just as well be offered by, say, one's wife or brother or by the members of a small study group. Without such personal contact the study of Steiner's work becomes much more difficult, it could become intellectual instead of being constantly enlivened by personal experience and observations. The personal conversation, on the other hand, offers real benefits. The more established anthroposophist has a new opportunity to clarify his thoughts and to revise them in the light of the unique human situation with which he is confronted, the newcomer can be encouraged to make the *next* step and to realise that his questions and doubts are justified and are of a more general validity and profundity than he himself had realised at first. Most of all, in the process of conversation new questions and insights arise, the origin of which lies neither in the one nor in the other, but in the mysterious interweaving of two wanderers on the path to the Spirit, to the Divine.

The Books

There are four major books by Rudolf Steiner which can be used as gateways to anthroposophy: *How to Attain Knowledge of Higher Worlds*, *Theosophy*, *Occult Science*, and *The Philosophy of Freedom*. The first of these gives advice to would-be meditants, both concerning some basic meditative exercises as well as for the ordering of the student's personal life. *Theosophy* and *Occult Science* give an account of Steiner's teaching as developed about 1910. While *Theosophy* describes certain basic features of man and the world, *Occult Science* looks at the same complex of facts from the point of view of development. The former book describes a static reality, the latter a universe in evolution. *The Philosophy of Freedom* is the final work and culmination of Steiner's philosophical thinking and preceded his theosophical and anthroposophical activities. It first discusses problems of cognition and ends with questions of freedom, of the responsibilities freely accepted that go with the life of modern man.

Yet none of these books is an introduction in the ordinary sense of the term. If I take an *Introduction to the Geography of Latin America* and read this book with reasonable intelligence, I expect in the end to know a good deal about the countries concerned. The study of Steiner's books demands more than intelligence. It needs constant inner activity. The books are not just for reading, each of them is a book of exercises. The more they are 'practised', the more the reader changes. This is quite obvious with *Knowledge of Higher Worlds*. Straightforward reading of the book will be of little help. Taking up one of the exercises and working with it regularly for, say, half a year, and introducing a few changes in one's life will provide the basis for *further* study. Activity and understanding, will, thought and the life of the soul will have to proceed more or less simultaneously.

The same holds good of the two books which attempt to describe in outline the world of man and the world of the spirit, *Theosophy* and *Occult Science*, and is equally true of the *Philosophy of Freedom*. If we read these books like good novels little will remain in our mind. If we read them like textbooks we shall retain some abstract facts which we may learn to use and play about with, but which will never give us any real understanding of the world of the spirit. Only if we learn to follow Steiner's train of thought so carefully that we ourselves can rethink a whole chapter, only if we are able to lay aside our book after we have read a paragraph and quietly mull over its content can we hope to enter into Steiner's teaching with any real understanding.

In particular, it is important to learn to suspend our judgement. Any discoverer of a new land has incredible stories to tell: the midday sun stands in the North, the people of Cathay burn paper money. Also the inner world has its unexpected surprises. All through his work Steiner gives descriptions of the being of man in his spiritual-physical totality. Few of these descriptions are identical, some seem even to contradict each other. It all depends on the direction from which you approach a certain reality. Steiner often uses the image of a tree standing in its natural surrounding. It will look very different to two observers approaching it from different directions. Yet after a few words the two will recognise that they have seen the same object. From particle physics we know how the 'objective' reality can never be described, the approach of the observer is bound to bring about a change in the facts observed. The same difficulty is encountered by the sociologist. He too, by his very presence, will change the world he attempts to describe.

We cannot enter into realms of meaning without bringing a relational element into play. Steiner is, of course, well aware of this fact and tries to counter it in two ways. He endeavours to make himself as objective an observer as is humanly possible, and he attempts to describe the same reality from ever new vantage points.

To sum up: to approach Steiner through a study of his books needs more than good will and intelligence. These books do not only present completely new facts, they also provide a spiritual training. Suspension of judgement must be coupled with critical discernment, clarity of thought with exercise in empathy in so far as the reader must be ready to re-create the development of his material, and he must further be ready to absorb emotionally what he has read and integrate it with his own experiences, insights and certainties.

The Lectures

There are a few thousand lectures which Steiner gave. Some of them are known only from fragmentary notes taken during or after the lectures, but in the course of time the quality of these notes increased so that most of the later lectures seem near perfect. They vary immensely in character and style. One or two of the earlier lecture courses[4] are most suitable for the newcomer as they provide a fairly easy introduction to Steiner's views during the 'theosophical' period. Others as for instance The Manifestations of Karma or From Jesus to Christ[5], provide an approach to a special part of Steiner's teaching. Some lectures are as demanding as the books, others are easier because of their more personal approach. So it should be quite possible to find among them some which make a special appeal to a particular reader.

This relative ease of approach is, however, balanced by the fact that each of these lecture courses or single lectures lacks the 'objective' presentation of the books. The lectures can only be truly appreciated if they are seen as unique communications between Rudolf Steiner and a particular group of people.

In an earlier chapter we tried to envisage the real nature of these lectures. (See The Lecturer: an Appendix.) They were spiritual acts of a unique kind. So we need only remind ourselves here that Steiner lived simultaneously in three relationships: in his immediate awareness of a particular being or beings in spiritual worlds, in his equally immediate relationship with his audience, and his conscious feeling for the cultural and political events in the world beyond the lecture room. Often the subject of a lecture was chosen by the people whom Steiner addressed, sometimes he dealt with contemporary events, sometimes he had to adjust social difficulties and tensions within a group of people, sometimes a lecture was specifically conceived for the benefit of a single member of the audience. Some of the lectures reach most profound depths equal to the greatest religious or philosophical documents of mankind. Occasionally it might seem that either his penetration into spiritual realms was at this occasion incomplete or that he felt strong inner resistance on the part of his audience and so he did not fully communicate what appeared to his inner eye.

A discerning reader will find in this superabundance of lectures plenty of material which is suited to his particular needs and expectations, but unless he is aware of the unique way in which each lecture came about he might make the mistake of generalising what is a particular, but nevertheless totally valid, insight into spiritual realities.

The Verses

There exist a large number of verses which Steiner composed, many of which are available in English translations.[6] Occasionally he summed up the content of a lecture in a few mantric lines. At other occasions he formed the lecture around a verse. Many of the extant verses were written for a particular person to give him or her advice, strength or direction and to be the subject for his or her personal meditation. In each verse a small area of Steiner's insights becomes manifest, not only through its content, but also through musical and poetical values. Choice of words, metre and rhythm, traces of rhyme and alliteration, the qualities of the sounds employed, they all act together and appeal simultaneously to our understanding and our emotional sensitivities. As with the lectures, the verses too offer a great variety of subjects and styles of presentation, and so many a person will find among them what for him is a jewel, something which, after a short span of time, he will know by heart, something which will accompany him through his working day and to which he will turn in quiet hours of contemplation. So he will very gradually penetrate ever more profoundly into the world of Steiner's experience, knowing full well that each verse offers but one particular glimpse into the world in which Steiner moved about freely as one of its rightful denizens.

A Question of Language

With these verses the question of translation arises in its most acute form. Steiner handles the German language with great freedom, and sometimes strained it in order to say what by its very nature can hardly be expressed in human language. What is difficult for the reader of German is sometimes impossible in English. So the recent translators of Steiner's books and lectures learned to recreate the original meaning in a form congenial to English-speaking people. This can only be done if the translator is prepared to completely recast, not only sentences, but, if necessary, a whole paragraph. It would be invidious to pick out one particular translator active now, so we take as *one* example of a truly felicitous translation *The Redemption of Thinking*[7] by the late Canon Shepherd.

For their meditative work Steiner gave to his pupils existing formulations in Sanskrit, Hebrew, Greek, Latin, German and English. But, as far as we are aware, he composed his own verses only in his native German. So the translator is faced with the question of preserving all the German musical values in a meaningful translation. Here he has but two choices. To attempt to preserve the literal meaning as far as this is possible without violating the genius of English poetry. Or as Owen Barfield did in *The Year Participated*[8] completely to dissolve the German poem and build out of its elements an entirely new weft of words consonant with the expressive possibilities of the English language. Each element of the original is preserved, both in explicit content and in implicit values, but the body of English which conveys the original meaning wins in power and beauty when compared with other good translations. For the English-speaking student who wishes to live with some of Steiner's verses two possibilities present themselves. He either familiarises himself with the translation that seems best to him or her, or one acquires a literal word-for-word translation and then works with the German original. This is, of course, the more laborious way, but in the end is likely to lead further. After all, the German anthroposophist too will, as stated above, use some meditative formulations in a non-German language.

Obstacles

The main obstacle that stands in our way to Steiner lies in us, in the way the scientific climate of the last centuries has conditioned our mind. Steiner endeavours to make us aware of the development of human consciousness and to encourage us to make the next great leap forward. Many of us fail in this respect, at least in the beginning. But as long as this leap has not been achieved we fail to do justice to Steiner. Colin Wilson is a good example of a writer who wishes to penetrate into Steiner's ideas, but is unable to appreciate them from inside as it were.[9] Others less critical are attracted by one aspect of Steiner's work or another, and decide to 'believe' him. But this was just an attitude which Steiner did his best to discourage.

He hoped that there would arise a significant number of people able to re-think and to re-experience some of his investigations into the Spirit. The present writer thinks that this is very difficult to achieve until one or two experiences become a reality to us, experiences which are at variance with what is generally taken for granted in our age.

As long as I look at the world with an 'observer consciousness' I cannot genuinely share Steiner's world. The 'world' is outside me, I look at it coolly and 'objectively', and have my private and totally irrelevant human reactions. As any nuclear physicist and any sociologist will confirm this is not so. The presence of an observer changes the observed world. As many an engaged man or woman will agree the stance of observer-cum-manipulator has terribly endangered our world. Our planet is threatened, our society fractured. The 'observer-consciousness' is both untrue and dangerous. Unless I feel part of the whole world, made out of the same stuff as the universe, unless I feel the relevance of my inner non-physical being, its importance for the future and its kinship with the unseen world beyond me, as for instance Blake and Wordsworth experienced it, – Steiner will speak to me from outside. But if I can once share in this mode of experience I can develop and refine it. Through devoted hearing and seeing I learn to communicate with other beings on earth, and through meditation with spiritual beings. Then, – and only then – shall I know the world of which Steiner speaks.

But there are two further obstacles in our approach to Rudolf Steiner. The one is the man himself, the other the anthroposophists whom we may encounter. Rittelmeyer, from whom we quoted extensively in the second chapter of this book, was perhaps the first to face this difficulty openly and honestly. Great men – he speaks of 'leaders of mankind' – are few and far between, and we must take them as they come. But here we are not referring to this or that idiosyncracy which Steiner may have displayed, but to three objective factors which can sometimes stand in the way between Steiner and the English-speaking reader of today.

There is first Steiner's concreteness. Those of us who are used to the language of the Church or Chapel as well as those familiar with Eastern sages can be puzzled, at first, by the definite nature of many – but by no means all – of Rudolf Steiner's statements about the world of the spirit. Compared to some other teachers' Steiner's presentation is often cool. We have to remind ourselves that these are non-physical facts which are related to us, so clear can be the outlines in which the picture is drawn. The reader of this book will understand the two main reasons behind this way of presentation. The unemotional, 'objective' attitude distances the writer from the reader and thereby emphasises the spiritual independence of the latter, the concrete nature of the facts communicated allows him to use on his own responsibility what he has been told and thereby change not only himself, but also the world around him.

Many a Western reader becomes conscious of a Germanic streak in Steiner. Everything seems so very orderly and tidy. To some people he appears pedantic, but C. S. Lewis, one of his more important critics, finds this cool and orderly presentation encouraging when he compares it to the 'white-hot' occultism which he met in Britain. But *is* Steiner really so cool, pedantic and 'German' as some of his readers feel? Is he really the man who reveals himself thus or is it the way he chose to address particular audiences? If any earnest reader feels this attitude is a *real* obstacle he would be advised to make a systematic study of Steiner's lectures in England and Wales, or in Sweden or in Austria. He might also like to look into the lectures to workmen which we mentioned above. In all these different lectures he will meet a completely different style of presentation, possibly more in harmony with her or his own expectations. One could also start by concentrating on Steiner's last phase, particularly the period after the foundation of the Anthroposophical Society. These courses are, however, not always easy to study.

The most serious obstacle is the third, our distance from Steiner in time. In one respect, and this is a most important fact, his work is much more relevant to our age than it was to people in Edwardian times. We *know* what he is talking about, the social and spiritual facts of the end of this century. To people at the beginning of the century his message was often but an interesting story. The difficulty lies somewhere else. Steiner had to translate the fruits of his inner vision into concepts with which his audience was more or less familiar. If he spoke to us today he would choose not only different terms, but also refer to totally new areas in the study of human and animal psychology, astrophysics, geomorphology, ecology, etc., which might have served his purpose much better than the scientific and cultural situation of his day. Also many of the subjects he treated were suggested by his audiences or necessitated by the events of the day. Some of these subjects have no longer the same relevance to us today and so it is necessary consciously to allow for the passing of time and, occasionally ask ourselves: how would Steiner have tackled the same subject today?

The Flow of Time

Steiner himself was very much aware of this problem. More than most people of his age he had a strong feeling for the reality of time and for a world in constant evolution. What he said was said not only to particular groups of people, but also for particular situations. He went so far as to suggest to the teachers of the *Waldorfschule* that they should rewrite his basic books for the new generation. This was about fifteen years after the appearance of these books. Now 75 years have passed. Why has Rudolf Steiner's suggestion not been acted on?

Anthroposophists: Autocracy, Idolisation and Intellectualism

This brings us to the second set of obstacles: many anthroposophists have failed to take up Rudolf Steiner's impulses. To understand this tragic fact we must look at the situation of Steiner's contemporaries. They largely stemmed from well-to-do families with a traditional outlook. Faced with a man whom they felt to be infinitely superior to themselves they not only looked up to, but even idolised him. To live a 'righteous' sort of life many adopted habits and attitudes copied from the great man himself. That he, the author of *The Philosophy of Freedom*, wanted to make them creative, independent and truly authentic people they were – many of them – unable to see. That he spoke up for a new social order radically different from the capitalist society in which they – most of them – felt thoroughly at home was a matter of real sorrow to them. They in turn built up a Society with strong autocratic tendencies while Steiner himself remained outside this society.

At the same time this first generation of anthroposophists related themselves in a particular way to the statements Steiner made. He himself wanted to be taken seriously, but was overjoyed when this attitude was coupled with critical detachment and responsible weighing of the evidence. This attitude he found particularly pleasing in Friedrich Rittelmeyer. Against this, the majority of his followers were, understandably, filled with total trust in a man of undoubted charisma. So they were inclined to take each statement he made as gospel, the truth which needed no examination. If Steiner described a fact in a particular way it followed that anybody else who looked differently at the same complex was certainly wrong, perhaps even malicious.

Now there are cases where Steiner was right and practically all his contemporaries mistaken. But usually his statements throw a new light on the fact without completely invalidating what other competent people had said. Sometimes the cautious reader will ask himself whether Steiner in the face of so much conflicting evidence could be right.

If we look at every statement Steiner made as a message of the spiritual world we endow Steiner with greater authority than that assumed by the Roman Pope. If we fail to see how certain ideas of his have their root in the general climate of the time and sometimes stem from definite people, if we do not account for the fact that like any other human being Steiner was to a certain degree shaped by his environment and that he like any other human being had some prejudices, had not studied everything and, as repeatedly stated above, made many of his statements to particular groups of people and in a unique situation, never to be repeated, we turn a living man into an idol. One can, if one is so inclined, worship an idol. A real man with all his faults and weaknesses can be loved. There are few people more worthy of love than Steiner.

A third feature which goes back to the days of the Theosophical Society is the fact that many anthroposophists see the aim of their study in relating one statement of Steiner's to one or more other statements which he made. In this way new connections are found, often interesting and revealing, but the whole endeavour remains a network of thoughts. This is, of course, one way of working with Steiner's statements, and one certainly sanctioned by him. But it is only *one* way. If we make it our habit to link Steiner's statements to the evidence of facts, to questions of our moral and spiritual existence, to our own modest spiritual experiences Anthroposophy will no longer be an intellectual exercise, but will spring to life.

These three tendencies, autocracy, idolisation and intellectualism featured to a certain degree in the life of the Theosophical Society and the early Anthroposophical Society.

When Steiner founded the new Anthroposophical Society as described in the previous chapter only a minority of anthroposophists saw what he had really intended. So traditions which had their origin as far back as the Theosophical Society were continued. Newcomers often felt oppressed by these traditions and either did not join the Society or played little part in it or were gradually moulded to traditionalists themselves. However, the number of those who feel kindled by the full compass of Rudolf Steiner's impulse, who are committed to spiritual development, social renewal and individual responsibility and creativity is growing all the time. They are opposed to any 'anthroposophic church', a hierarchic structure with definite opinions and a uniform style of life. They cannot forget that Rudolf Steiner clearly stated in the 'Statutes' which he gave to the Society that there was no place in it for dogmatism and sectarianism. This means, however, that in an utterly free society they can only set an example. They cannot say to their fellow members: your form of anthroposophy is not the right one. If the house of Anthroposophy cannot contain many mansions it will collapse. But it is nevertheless true that where anthroposophical groups or institutions still persist in traditional and parochial ways they are building up the greatest obstacle which faces many a newcomer kindled by the totality of Rudolf Steiner's impulse.

Footnotes

Wherever possible an English translation of books in German is quoted, but the reader should note that the text of the source given might slightly differ from that found in this volume as the author specially translated most of the relevant passages.

Difficulties arise about Steiner's letters (*Briefe.*) The early letters from which we quote were originally published in two volumes. Usually the first volume is quoted in the current, the third edition. The same edition has not brought out the second volume, so we quote the original edition. But the first edition included in its first volume also an autobiographical lecture which so far does not seem to have been published again. So we have to quote the first edition as well and this is always noted.

Then there are a number of letters which in the original edition appeared in the first volume, but will in future be found in the second. Quotations of these letters refer to the date of writing and to the recipient of the letter.

Chapter One

1. RS Lecture, Helsinki 11.4.12. Steiner, *Der Zusammenhang*.
2. RS Lecture, Berlin 4.2.13. Steiner, *Briefe i*, first edition p.11.
3. R. Steiner, *Briefe i*, p.208.
4. R. Steiner, *Briefe i*, p.110.
5. E. Bock, p.407f.
6. RS Lecture, Berlin 4.2.13. Steiner, *Briefe i*, first edition p.34.
7. E. Bock, p.43.
8. F. Eckstein, pp.130f.
9. RS Letter to Rosa Mayreder 20.5.91.
10. RS Letter to Rosa Mayreder 12.3.91.
11. RS Letter to Ladislaus Specht 3.1.91.
12. R. Steiner, *From Symptom to Reality*, p.142.
13. J. Muecke and A. Rudolph, pp.45,49,56,82.
14. R. Steiner, *Mysticism at the Dawn of the Modern Age* and *Christianity as a Mystical Fact*.
15. RS Letter to Pauline Specht 12.3.91.
16. RS Letter 21.7.02.
17. RS Lecture, London 24.8.24. Steiner, *Die Konstitution*.

18. RS Letter to Wilhelm Huebbe-Schleiden 16.8.02.
19. Ibid.
20. R. Steiner, *From Symptom to Reality*, p.151.
21. cf. Bibliography.
22. Poeppig, *Rudolf Steiner*, pp.247f.
23. H. Biesantz and A. Klingborg, pp.16f.
24. cf. H. Biesantz and A. K'ingborg.
25. cf. The famous Lansdowne letter in the *Daily Telegraph*, November 1917.
26. A. Freeman and C. Waterman, *The Golden Blade 1958*, p.58.
27. R. Steiner, *Konferenzen*.
28. R. Steiner, *An Autobiography*.
    The Life, Nature and Cultivation of Anthroposophy.
    Anthroposophical Leading Thoughts.

Chapter Two

1. There are a number of accounts of encounters and experiences with Rudolf Steiner in his maturity. Fortunately, one of the best is available in English: Rittelmeyer, *Rudolf Steiner Enters my Life*. The author was an eminent Protestant preacher and theologian. Another outstanding account, written in Stalin's Russia, is by Andrei Bely, the great Russian poet. It is quoted from the German translation, *Verwandeln des Lebens*.
2. R. Steiner, *Wahrspruchworte*, p.269. The English translation was made for this book by Owen Barfield, to whom special thanks are due.
3. Lecture, Berlin 4.2.13. Steiner, *Briefe i*, first edition pp.18f.
4. Letter to Pauline and Ladislaus Specht 30.9.90.
5. A. Turgenieff, pp.50f.
6. E. Lehrs, pp.191f.
7. A. Keyserlingk, p.94.
8. A. Bely, pp.42-66, 82ff.
9. E. Leinhas, pp.150f.
10. A. Bely, p.108.
11. Poeppig, *Vermächtnis*, pp.170f.
12. E. Leinhas, pp.22f.
13. Poeppig, *Vermächtnis*, pp.170f.
14. A. Bely, p.125.
15. F. Rittelmeyer, p.114.
16. F. Rittelmeyer, p.117.
17. F. Rittelmeyer, pp.34f.
18. Poeppig, *Rudolf Steiner*, p.64.

19. F. Rittelmeyer, pp.147f.
20. E. Leinhas, pp.46f.
21. A. Bely, pp.390f.
22. F. Rittelmeyer, p.132.
23. *Magazine Info 3*, October 1985, p.11.
24. A. Turgenieff, p.79.
25. E. Lehrs, p.327.
26. F. Rittelmeyer, pp.88f.
27. A. Bely, pp.217f.
28. A. Bely, pp.218f.
29. A. Bely, pp.83f.
30. A. Bely, p.34.
31. Poeppig, *Vermächtnis*, p.156.
32. E. Lehrs, p.303.
33. F. Rittelmeyer, p.58.
34. F. Rittelmeyer, pp.71f.
35. F. Rittelmeyer, p.114.
36. Ibid.
37. F. Rittelmeyer, pp.118f.
38. F. Rittelmeyer, pp.62f.
39. F. Rittelmeyer, pp.45ff.
40. A. Bely, p.78.
41. A. Bely, pp.79f.
42. A. Samweber, pp.20f.
43. F. Rittelmeyer, p.77.
44. A. Samweber, p.38.
45. A. Samweber, p.39.
46. F. Rittelmeyer, pp.104ff.
47. A. Samweber, pp.23f.
48. W. Kugler, p.223.
49. A. Bely, pp.148f.
50. R. Steiner, *Philosophy, Cosmology, Religion*, p.120.
51. R. Steiner, *Inneres Wesen*, p.70.
52. R. Steiner, *The Gospel of St John*, pp.21ff.
53. R. Steiner, *Mitteleuropa zwischen Ost und West*, pp.270.
54. R. Steiner, *The Gospel of St John*, p.23.
55. R. Steiner, *From Symptom to Reality*, p.184.
56. A. Bely, pp.436-439, 455-458.
57. H. Müller, p.32.
58. R. Steiner, *Die geistigen Hintergründe*, p.52.

59. F. Rittelmeyer, p.66.
60. A. Bely, p.153.
61. A. Bely, p.154.

Chapter Three

1. See bibliography.
2. RS *Briefe i*, p.110.
3. RS *Briefe i*, first edition p.18.
4. See also O. Barfield, *The Case*.
5. R. Steiner, *From Symptom to Reality*, p.136.
6. R. Steiner, *Universe, Earth and Man*.
7. E. Lehrs, p.321.

Chapter Four

1. R. Steiner, *Inner Realities of Evolution*.

Chapter Five

1. RS Letter to Rosa Mayreder, 22.12.91.
2. RS *Briefe ii*, first edition p.89.
3. RS *Briefe ii*, first edition p.181.
4. R. Steiner, *An Autobiography*, pp.318ff.
5. R. Steiner, *The Gospel of St John*, p.128.
6. R. Steiner, *The Festivals*, p.180.
7. R. Steiner, *The Gospel of St Luke*, p.94.
8. R. Steiner, *Notwendigkeit und Freiheit*, p.166.
9. C. Hill, *The World Turned Upside Down*.

Chapter Six

1. See bibliography.
2. R. Steiner, *Occult Science*, pp.228ff, *Knowledge of Higher Worlds*, p.63ff.
3. See bibliography.
4. See bibliography.
5. See bibliography.
6. R. Steiner, *Knowledge of the Higher Worlds*, and *Esoteric Development*.

Chapter Seven

1. R. Steiner, *Threefolding*.
2. See bibliography for A. C. Harwood, F. Carlgren, B. Masters.
3. For more detail see bibliography, Lievegoed.
4. A. Bittleston and D. Jones, editors, *The Golden Blade 1984*, pp.117ff.
5. See bibliography, S. Leber.
6. T. Weihs, *Children in Need of Special Care*.
7. J. Huber, *Astral-Marx*.

Chapter Eight

1. See bibliography, D. Bruell.
2. R. Steiner, *Spiritual Ground of Education*.
3. R. Steiner, *Threefolding*.
4. See bibliography, Polzer-Hoditz.
5. L. Polzer-Hoditz, pp.505ff, 520, 535f.
6. R. Steiner, *Towards Social Renewal*.
7. R. Steiner, *World Economy*.
8. R. Steiner, *The Social Future*.

Chapter Nine

1. R. Grosse, *The Christmas Foundation*.
2. R. Steiner, *Life, Nature, and Cultivation of Anthroposophy*, p.1.
3. Op. cit. p.27.
4. R. Steiner, *Die Weihnachtstagung*, p.108.
5. R. Steiner, *Life, Nature*, p.7.
6. Op. cit. p.43.

Chapter Ten

1. See bibliography, L. Adey.
2. L. Adey, p.25.
3. R. Steiner, *Arbeitervorträge*.
4. R. Steiner, *The Theosophy of the Rosicrucians*, and *At the Gates of Spiritual Science*.
5. See bibliography.
6. R. Steiner, *Verses and Meditations*.
7. See bibliography.
8. O. Barfield, *The Year Participated*.
9. See bibliography.

Bibliography

The standard edition of Rudolf Steiner's works is published by Rudolf Steiner Verlag, Dornach, Switzerland. Most of the English translations are published either by Rudolf Steiner Press, London or by Anthroposophical Press, Spring Valley, New York. Below, these three companies will be referred to as Dornach, London and Spring Valley respectively.

L. Adey, *C. S. Lewis's Great War with Owen Barfield*, University of Victoria, Canada 1978.

O. Barfield, *The Case for Anthroposophy*, London 1970.

O. Barfield, *The Year Participated*, London 1985.

A. Belyi, *Verwandeln des Lebens*, Zbinden Verlag, Basel 1975.

H. Biesantz and A. Klingborg, *The Goetheanum. Rudolf Steiner's Architectural Impulse*, London 1979.

A. Bittleston and D. Jones, *The Golden Blade 1984*, Forest Row, Sussex.

E. Bock, *Rudolf Steiner*, Verlag Freies Geistesleben, Stuttgart 1961.

D. Bruell, *Der anthroposophische Sozialimpuls*, Novalis Verlag, Schaffhausen 1984.

R. Bruell, *Info 3*, a magazine edited by R. Bruell, Frankfurt.

V. Bukovsky, *To Build a Castle*.

F. Carlgren, *Education Towards Freedom*, Lanthorn Press, East Grinstead, Sussex 1976.

F. Eckstein, *Alte Unnennbare Tage*, Herbert Reichner Verlag, Wien 1936.

A. Freeman and C. Waterman, *The Golden Blade 1958*, Forest Row, Sussex.

R. Grosse, The Christmas Foundation, Steiner Book Centre, Vancouver 1984.

A. C. Harwood, *The Recovery of Man in Childhood*, Spring Valley 1982.

C. Hill, *The World Turned Upside Down*, Penguin, Harmondsworth 1975.

J. Huber, *Astral-Marx*, article in Kursbuch no. 55, March 1979.

A. Keyserlingk, *Koberwitz 1924*, Hilfswerk Elisabeth, Stuttgart 1974.

W. Kugler, *Rudolf Steiner und die Anthroposophie*, Dumont Verlag, Köln 1980.

S. Leber, *Die Waldorfschule und ihr soziales Umfeld*, Verlag Freies Geistesleben, Stuttgart.

E. Lehrs, *Gelebte Erwartung*, Mellinger Verlag, Stuttgart 1979.

E. Leinhas, *Aus der Arbeit mit Rudolf Steiner*, Zbinden Verlag, Basel 1950.

B. S. J. Lievegoed, *Phases*, Rudolf Steiner Press, London 1982.

B. Masters, *Child and Man*, Steiner Schools Fellowship, Forest Row, Sussex.

J. Muecke and A. Rudolph, *Erinnerungen an Rudolf Steiner*, Zbinden Verlag, Basel 1979.

H. Müller, *Spuren auf dem Weg*, Mellinger Verlag, Stuttgart 1976.

F. Poeppig, *Heiliges Vermächtnis*, R. Geering Verlag, Basel 1938.

F. Poeppig, *Rudolf Steiner*, Verlag Bettina Woiczik, Wien 1960.

L. Polzer-Hoditz, *Kaiser Karl*, Putnam 1928. Vienna 1980.

F. Rittelmeyer, *Rudolf Steiner Enters my Life*, Floris Books, Edinburgh 1982.

A. Samweber, *Aus meinem Leben*, Verlag die Pforte, Basel 1981.

E. Schiller, *Rudolf Steiner and Initiation*, Spring Valley 1981.

R. Steiner, *Anthroposophical Leading Thoughts*, London 1985.

R. Steiner, *Arbeitervorträge*, 8 vols, Dornach 1976.

R. Steiner, *At the Gates of Spiritual Science*, London 1976.

R. Steiner, *An Autobiography*, Steinerbooks, Blauvelt, New York 1980.

R. Steiner, *Briefe*, 2 vols, first edition, Dornach 1953.

R. Steiner, *Briefe*, vol i, third edition, Dornach 1985.

R. Steiner, *Christianity as a Mystical Fact*, London 1972.

R. Steiner, *Conferences with the Teachers of the Waldorf School*, Steiner Schools Fellowship Publications, Forest Row, Sussex 1986.

R. Steiner, *Esoteric Development*, Spring Valley 1982.

R. Steiner, *The Festivals and their Meaning*, London 1981.

R. Steiner, *From Jesus to Christ*, London 1976.

R. Steiner, *From Symptom to Reality in Modern History*, London 1976.

R. Steiner, *Die geistigen Hintergründe des ersten Weltkriegs*, Dornach 1974.

R. Steiner, *Goethe's World View*, Mercury Press, Spring Valley, New York 1985.

R. Steiner, *The Gospel of St John and its Relationship to the Other Gospels*, Spring Valley 1982.

R. Steiner, *The Gospel of St Luke*, London 1975.

R. Steiner, *Inneres Wesen des Menschen und Leben zwischen Tod und neuer Geburt*, Dornach 1959.

R. Steiner, *Inner Realities of Evolution*, London 1953.

R. Steiner, *Knowledge of the Higher Worlds*, London 1985.

R. Steiner, *Konferenzen mit den Lehrern der Waldorfschule*, 3 vols, Dornach 1985.

R. Steiner, *Die Konstitution der Allgemeinen Anthroposophischen Gesellschaft*, Dornach 1966.

R. Steiner, *Manifestations of Karma*, London 1984.

R. Steiner, *The Life, Nature and Cultivation of Anthroposophy*, London 1963.

R. Steiner, *Mitteleuropa zwischen Ost und West*, Dornach 1971.

R. Steiner, *Mysticism at the Dawn of the Modern Age*, Steinerbooks, Blauvelt, New York 1980.

R. Steiner, *Occult Science*, London 1984.

R. Steiner, *Philosophy, Cosmology and Religion*, Spring Valley 1984.

R. Steiner, *The Philosophy of Freedom*, London 1984.

R. Steiner, *Practical Training in Thought*, Spring Valley 1985.

R. Steiner, *The Redemption of Thinking*, Spring Valley 1985.

R. Steiner, *The Social Future*, Spring Valley 1972.

R. Steiner, *The Spiritual Ground of Education*, London 1947.

R. Steiner, *A Theory of Knowledge*, Spring Valley 1978.

R. Steiner, *Theosophy*, Spring Valley 1985.

R. Steiner, *Theosophy of the Rosicrucians*, London 1981.

R. Steiner, *Threefolding, A Social Alternative*, London 1980.

R. Steiner, *Towards Social Renewal*, London 1977.

R. Steiner, *Truth and Knowledge*, Steinerbooks, Blauvelt, New York 1981.

R. Steiner, *Universe, Earth and Man*, London 1955.

R. Steiner, *Verses and Meditations*, London 1985.

R. Steiner, *Wahrspruchworte*, Dornach 1981.

R. Steiner, *Die Weihnachtstagung zur Begründung der Allgemeinen Anthroposophischen Gesellschaft*, Dornach 1985.

R. Steiner, *World Economy*, London 1977.

R. Steiner, *Der Zusammenhang des Menschen mit der elementarischen Welt*, Dornach 1968.

A. Turgenieff, *Erinnerungen an Rudolf Steiner*, Verlag Freies Geistesleben, Stuttgart 1972.

T. Weihs, *Children in Need of Special Care*, Souvenir Press, London 1984.

C. Wilson, *Rudolf Steiner, The Man and his Vision*, Aquarian Press, Wellingborough 1985.

DYING FORESTS
A crisis in consciousness.
Transforming our way of life.
46 colour pictures and text by Jochen Bockemühl.
Introduction by Professor Brian Goodwin.
Translated by John Meeks.

Forests are dying in central Europe – many trees are dying in the Swiss mountains, threatening erosion problems. Many lakes in Scandinavia, Scotland and North Wales now have no fish. Sulphur dioxide, ozone, nitric oxides from industry, traffic and power stations are some causes. But what part do people play in causing forest die-back?

Dying Forests offers the insights of Jochen Bockemühl – both scientist and artist – into the underlying causes of forest die-back. These causes relate closely to our modern life style and our destructive forms of thinking and ways of exploiting nature. The author, by means of his water colour sketches and commentary, describes how, through the development of a sensitive observation of landscape ecology, a more conscious encounter with nature can take place. Through the exercises described in **Dying Forests**, the strength to change one's habits and our destructive technology may emerge. **Dying Forests** is a striking example of the use of Goethe's scientific method which aims to understand the living whole, rather than the dead parts.

Jochen Bockemühl is a scientist working at the Goetheanum Research Laboratory in Dornach, Switzerland. He has lectured and conducted many 'observation workshops' in the English speaking world. His work on plant metamorphosis is included in Open University biology course texts.

Sewn limp bound; full colour cover; 8¼" x 8¼" (210 x 210mm); 96pp; 46 water colour illustrations in full colour, plus drawings. ISBN 1 869 890 02 7

VISION IN ACTION
The art of taking and shaping initiatives.
Christopher Schaefer and Tijno Voors.

Vision is a working book for those involved in taking and shaping initiatives. The authors ask:- How can individuals and groups take initiatives successfully? Once started, how can projects be shaped and developed effectively?

Building on their practical experience of fostering and taking initiatives, the authors offer useful road maps to those developing ventures. Examples are given of community projects, schools, employment initiatives, small businesses, farms, cultural and therapeutic centres.

The road maps include:-
The process of starting and nurturing initiatives;
Ways of working together;
Financing initiatives;
The development phases of initiatives;

Initiatives and individual development.

There are exercises, case studies and questionnaires which can be used by people preparing and reviewing initiatives, or considering their next step.

Christopher Schaefer PhD works in social and community development in the USA. Tijno Voors works at the centre for Social Development at Emerson College, Sussex.

Sewn limp bound; 8¼" x 5¼" (210 x 135mm); 190pp; 3 illustrations.
Not for sale in the USA.
ISBN 0 950 706 29 9

HOPE, EVOLUTION AND CHANGE
John Davy.
Introduction by Owen Barfield.

The twenty-seven articles in this book reflect the author's work as a scientist, journalist and lecturer: articles on evolutionary questions, language, education, science, caring for the planet, life after life, and contemporary thinkers like Schumacher and Elizabeth Kübler-Ross.

Colin Wilson '...a significant figure...' review of **Hope** in **Resurgence**.

Paperback; 8¼" x 5¼" (210 x 135mm); 274pp.
ISBN 0 950 706 27 2
To be published in German.

MAN ON THE THRESHOLD
The challenge of inner development.
Bernard Lievegoed, MD.

The author of **Phases** and **Developing Organisations** describes the challenge of inner development today. Eastern and western meditative paths are described, and there are sections on personal development and counselling.

Paperback; full colour cover; 8¼" x 5¼" (210 x 135mm); 224pp.
ISBN 0 950 706 26 4

SOCIAL ECOLOGY
Exploring post-industrial society.
Martin Large.

Social Ecology looks at the development of individuals, groups, organisations and society in the post-industrial age.

Paperback; 8¼" x 5¾" (210 x 145mm); 162pp.
ISBN 0 950 706 22 1

ARIADNE'S AWAKENING
Taking up the threads of consciousness.
Signe Schaefer, Betty Staley and Margli Matthews.

Much has been written about women and men in terms of rôles, gender and social forms through the ages. The past two decades have witnessed widespread change in 'rights' and 'equality' on external levels, but this has not always made for more human fulfilment. The authors acknowledge the context of feminism, but broaden its picture enormously. They view 'masculine' and 'feminine' not just as bodily forms, but as principles of meaning: principles at work within each of us, in society and indeed in the entire span of Earth evolution.

Ariadne's Awakening traces through myth and history the journey humankind has made up to the present; it considers phases of life, relationships for men and women, and confronts such issues as the scientific management of conception and death, the rape of Earth's natural resources and the need for a New Feminine to influence values and decisions for the future.

Ariadne's Awakening is a book about understanding ourselves, and a search for a creative balance.

Signe Schaefer teaches at the Waldorf Institute, Spring Valley, New York. Margli Matthews teaches at Emerson College, Sussex and Betty Staley teaches in California. Signe and Margli were founder menbers of the Ariadne Women's Group, and wrote articles for **Lifeways**.

Sewn limp bound; 8¼" x 5¼" (210 x 135mm); 220pp approx.
ISBN 1 869 890 01 9
To be published in German.

MONEY, SOUL AND SPIRIT
Steve Briault and Glen Saunders.

Money is based on the authors' experience and insights gained through working with money in 'conventional' and 'alternative' settings, including the provision of community banking and advisory services to a wide range of individuals and organisations. Was D. H. Lawrence right when he wrote that money "poisons you when you've got it and starves you when you haven't"? How can we take hold of it in ways which support our bodily existence without enslaving our hearts and minds? How must we change our thinking, feeling and doing so that money can find its healthy place within the human community? The book does not offer tax advice, or tell you how to get rich: it takes its starting point from the fundamental questions people face today with the tremendous broadening of inner and outer choices. New spiritual directions, changing values in relationships, new attitudes to work and to working with others, a stronger sense of individual biography and personal development – all these indicate the context and the need for a change in our perspectives and approaches to money. This will be taken up for organisations, initiative groups and personal life.

Some of the themes covered will be:
managing and metamorphosing money;
possession – needs and wants;
humanising money – overcoming hypnosis and fear;
ensouling investment – savings and lending;
transforming work and payment;
welfare, charity, productivity;
inheritance and dependence.

Stephen Briault works at the Centre for Social Development at Emerson College. Glen Saunders is an accountant and works for Mercury Provident PLC.

Paperback; 8¼" x 5¼" (210 x 136mm); 160pp approx.
ISBN 0 860 890 07 8

ROCK BOTTOM
Beyond drug addiction.
By members of the Arta Rehabilitation Centre
Translated by Jakob Cornelius.

Drugs cause much debate, confusion and questions. People ask questions such as:-
Why do young people get into drugs?
What is addiction?
Which drugs are are there? How do they act?
What are the consequences of drug taking?

How can drug addicts be helped?
How can addiction be prevented?

Rock Bottom describes the work of *Arta*, a Dutch therapeutic community. The insights into the nature and causes of addiction, therapeutic methods and the meaning of addiction arise from this model of good practice.

Parents, teachers, social workers, doctors and counsellors will find **Rock Bottom** both a useful work book and a stimulus to fresh thinking about people facing drug problems.

Paperback; 8¼" x 5¼" (210 x 136mm); 92pp approx; photos and drawings.
ISBN 1 869 890 11 6

RECOGNITION OF REALITY
Reflections and prose poems.
Adam Curle.

Those of us living in the modern Western world (or 'North') have daily access to visual and factual images which travel with unprecedented rapidity from their place of origin to our newspaper page or television screen. Seemingly, these aim to 'inform' us about contemporary war, famine, poverty, summit meetings, human suffering, or other newsworthy events. How much of this we actually digest or comprehend is another matter. For many it is often enough to grapple with understanding our individual positions here and now, at this time, during this event or in this moment. And yet we are part of a wider world.

Adam Curle's mediation work over the past twenty-two years has taken him to international and personal situations of great tension, despair, hope, pain and change. Previous to and during this period he has been involved in problems of Third World development and has held professorships in psychology, education, development and peace studies at Exeter, Ghana, Harvard and Bradford Universities.

But in **Recognition of Reality** he chooses not to lecture. This is a book of reflections; glimpses of inner and outer worlds caught in poetic form and always based on true experience. At times gentle, at times painful, these pieces combine to offer our Age a compassionate interpretation of reality, and vision for the future. **Recognition of Reality** seeks to convey the essential truth and spiritual essence so often distorted or unseen amid human suffering and despair. Only by coming to terms with our fundamental being will we succeed in transforming and renewing this earth.

Paperback; 8¼" x 5¼" (210 x 136mm); 100pp approx; 67 poems.

THE CHILDREN'S YEAR
Crafts and clothes for children to make.
Stephanie Cooper, Christine Fynes-Clinton and Marye Rowling.

Here is a book which hopes to give the possibility to adults and children alike to rediscover the joy and satisfaction of making something that they know looks and feels good and which can also be played with imaginatively. It takes us through Spring, Summer, Autumn and Winter with appropriate gifts and toys to create, including full, clear instructions and illustrations. There is children's clothing as well, particularly meant to be made of natural fabrics to let the child's body breathe while growing. There are soft items for play and beauty, and there are firm solid wooden ones; moving toys such as balancing birds or climbing gnomes; horses which move when you add children to them! From woolly hats to play houses, mobiles or dolls, here are 112 potential treasures to make in seasonal groupings.

You needn't be an experienced crafts person to create something lovely, and the illustrations make it a joy to browse through while choosing what to make first. **The Children's Year** offers handwork for all ages and individualities, it reminds us of the process of creating as opposed to merely consuming, and all this in the context of nature's rhythm through the year.

The authors are parents who have tried and tested the things to make included in **The Children's Year**, with their own families.

Paperback or hardback; full colour cover; 10½" x 8½" (267mm x 216mm); 220pp; several hundred illustrations.
ISBN 1 869 890 00 0

FESTIVALS, FAMILY AND FOOD
Diana Carey and Judy Large.

'*Packed full of ideas on things to do, food to make, songs to sing and games to play, it's an invaluable resources book designed to help you and your family celebrate the various festival days scattered round the year.*'   The Observer

Paperback; full colour cover; 10" x 8" (250 x 200mm); 216pp; over 200 illustrations.
ISBN 0 950 706 23 X
Fourth impression.

LIFEWAYS
Working with family questions.
Gudrun Davy and Bons Voors.

Lifeways is about children, about family life, about being a parent. But most of all it is about freedom, and how the tension between family life and personal fulfilment can be resolved.